Secrets of Buying and Selling Real Estate . . .

Without Using Your Own Money!

ROBERT SHEMIN

WILEY

John Wiley & Sons, Inc.

Published by John Wiley & Sons, Inc., Hoboken, New Jersey.
Published simultaneously in Canada.

For general information on our other products and services please contact our Customer Care Department within the United States at (800) 762-2974, outside the United States at (317) 572-3993 or fax (317) 572-4002.

Wiley also publishes its books in a variety of electronic formats. Some content that appears in print may not be available in electronic books. For more information about Wiley products, visit our web site at www.Wiley.com.

Library of Congress Cataloging-in-Publication Data:

Shemin, Robert, 1963-
    Secrets of buying and selling real estate—without using your own money / Robert Shemin.
       p. cm.
    Includes index.
    ISBN 0-471-44924-5
    1. Mortgage loans—United States. 2. Real property—United States—Finance. 3. Real estate investment—United States—Finance. I. Title.

    HG2040.5.U5S525 2003
    332.7'2'0973—dc21

                                                                                2003053840

Printed in the United States of America

10 9 8 7 6 5 4 3

To Alexander. Know that as I write this and am away from you, I am thinking about you—Always and Forever.

CONTENTS

Contents

ACKNOWLEDGMENTS

Thanks to everyone at John Wiley & Sons, in particular Michael Hamilton, my forever patient and professional guide there, and his assistant, Kimberly Vaughn.

Barbara McNichol is more like a coauthor than an editor and always performs miracles cheerfully when working on my projects—thanks to Barbara and her assistant, Sherry Sterling.

My real estate speaking career is great thanks to Paul Bauer.

A special thanks to Wright Thurston, Mr. Landlord Ernie Kessler and especially Third Millennium Solutions—Jeff Vikari, Randy McKim, and Jason Halverson.

On a personal note, here's another to you Patricia—thanks for your patience. I am always grateful to my parents and family.

Thanks Jack Bufkin for being Jack Bufkin.

A special thanks to all of my students—your success is my goal. Good luck to you all. Tamera, thanks for lunch!

Property is the fruit of labor; property is desirable; it is a positive good in the world. That some should be rich shows that others may become rich and, hence, is just encouragement to industry and enterprise.
—ABRAHAM LINCOLN

I have written three best-selling books. My latest, *Unlimited Riches,* has quickly become one of the top real estate books in the United States.

Some people ask why I write books. At first, I wrote them to help myself. My first book answered the questions: How do you invest in real estate? How do you find deals? How do you lease-option? How are you making all this money? I found myself spending a lot of time telling people the same thing, so I wrote a report and told them to read it.

That's also why I started leading workshops—to bring people together twice a year so I could tell a lot of people, not just a few individuals, how to be successful real estate investors.

I love writing. I love teaching. I love helping people. It's fun, but where is the money? It's in real estate. Even though my books sell well, I made more money off one real estate deal in 2002 than from all of my book royalties in the past four years.

From a financial standpoint, I don't have to do any more real estate deals. But I keep involved because it's a blast. It's addictive. It's fun. And it's profitable. Yet the most satisfying aspect is helping other people. People say, "You helped me, and now my family has moved into a better house and we took some vacations. We're doing this!" Hearing that gives me unbelievable satisfaction.

At least once a year, I take one of my houses and pass it on to a homeless family. Why? Because I believe that, whatever we're doing, it's important to take some of our time—and some of our business—to help other people. I get the most satisfaction when I'm helping people get started, and watching them experience success as they go forward and help others. For me, there's nothing more rewarding.

I'm planting a seed for everyone reading this book—and especially for beginning investors—to help homeless families as you prosper in this business. (The best way is through a lease option. See Chapter 4, "Lease Optioning," for details.)

In December 2002, I gave away three houses anonymously. I've also gone on a talk show and given one away, and I want to do more. I publicize some of my home giveaways to inspire some of you to do the same. My goal is to see that no child in the United States ever has to live in a homeless shelter.

THINK ABOUT IT

If you increased your net worth by $1 million in the next seven years through real estate investing, what would you do with your new wealth?

I would buy _____

_____

I would help _____

_____

CHAPTER 1

Real estate is the closest thing to the proverbial pot of gold.
—ADA LOUISE HUXTABLE

Real Estate Is Not Real Estate: It's Creative Finance

The week I wrote this section, I bought and sold four properties. I closed on two in a single day and had three under contract for the following week. I'm a full-time real estate investor.

My job and your job is to find a deal and put it under contract. Learn all the ways to make money: buying real estate, creative finance, flipping properties, lease-optioning real estate, mortgage brokering, and money brokering. Then choose which way you like the best and run with it. Real estate is unique in that you can get into it without using any of your own money.

Have you ever tried to get in the stock market and make money? It can work; however, you have to buy a stock at the price it sells for on the day you buy. Let's say the price of a company's stock is $100 a share. If you want to buy it, you have to pay $100 and pray it goes up. If it goes to $120 in a year, you've made $20 for every $100 you spent on that stock. That's a 20 percent return on your investment, which is a good return.

You must be able to take into account that, historically, the stock market has between about a 9 and 13 percent annualized return—an average of 11 percent over the past 40 or 50 years. So if you're making 11 percent or more, you're doing great in the stock market. Unfortunately, for many, their stocks have gone down 10, 20, even 30 percent in the past few years.

However, to buy that $100 stock, you have to give the bank or brokerage firm (or whoever makes the transaction for you) a commission, plus you have to determine where that $100 comes from. If you have excellent credit, the brokerage may lend you half of the $100 and you still have to put up $50 of your own cash. That's what some people do when they invest in the stock market. Considering commissions and borrowing expenses, how much are you really making on the appreciation of that stock?

I recommend you consider investing in real estate for a better, long-term investment because of the features that make it unique, some of which follow.

What Makes Real Estate Unique

If you're serious about your money and serious about investing, you'll consider all the advantages of real estate investing that don't exist in other forms of investing.

Contract Real Estate for Less Than Its Value

Houses worth $100,000 can actually be found for $75,000 or $80,000. Some real estate worth $1 million can be found for $700,000; other properties worth $450,000 can be found for $350,000. You can contract to buy a property and control it immediately, even though you haven't given the seller money for it yet. Then, between 30 and 100 days later, you go to the closing and give the seller the agreed-upon price. You borrow money to pay for the property, then close on it, and, voilà, you own it.

Make an Infinite Return on Investment

If you find a house worth $1 million for $500,000 and your credit isn't great, there are some lenders who would lend you $500,000 for a property worth $1 million. In fact, they'd hope you'd miss a payment so they could take over the $1 million property for $500,000.

These lenders are called *hard moneylenders* (see Chapter 5, "Avenues Leading to Motivated Sellers," for more details). They don't pay attention to your credit; they care about the asset, the property itself, when they make their lending decisions. If it's 60 to 75 percent loan to value (see accompanying explanation), they might lend the funds regardless of your credit. Some of the big banks and mortgage companies make loans to people who have been in bankruptcy, who have made late payments, who have bad credit, and so on. They may still lend you 60 to 80 percent of the sale price on these properties. That's why you can find a property worth $100,000 and get it for $75,000, then borrow that $75,000 without putting your own money into the property. You rent the property for $1,000 a month, and your payment on the $75,000 you borrowed is $700 a month. After all of the expenses—taxes, insurance, vacancies, repairs, and overhead—you make some cash each month. Let's say you make $100 profit a month from the rent after paying all of the expenses. You've still invested zero in the property. Your return is infinite: $X for $0 invested.

Do you realize that this *wouldn't* work if you were buying stocks or gold or any other investment? With real estate, you potentially have an infinite

Loan to Value

Loan to value is a term used by real estate investors and lenders to indicate the ratio of debt or borrowed money compared to the value of a property.

If the house is worth $200,000 and the loan or mortgage is $200,000, then there is a 100 percent loan to value. Many conventional or regular lenders will lend 80 to 100 percent loan to value to home buyers who are going to live in the home. These are called *owner-occupied loans* since the loan is to someone who is going to live in the home. An *investor loan* is a loan to someone who is not going to live in the property. These loans are typically 65 to 85 percent loan to value. However, there are some 90 to 100 percent loan-to-value loans for investors.

All loans depend on three things: *collateral,* the value and type of asset or property; *credit,* the credit history of the borrower; and *income,* or the borrower's ability to repay the loan.

return on your investment. If you make only $1 because of unforeseen circumstances, your turnaround investment is still infinite because none of your own money is invested.

Real Estate Appreciates

Stocks certainly don't appreciate every year, especially if they're affected by an accounting scandal such as those experienced by Enron or MCI WorldCom in 2001–2002. Stocks can go from $80 a share down to $1 a share or less while, in most areas, real estate appreciates from 4 to 6 percent a year. It goes up even more in certain hot markets. Investing in real estate can bring you the greatest gains in your life if you can hang in there and stick it out. Think about what real estate in

THINK ABOUT IT

You make most of your money in real estate when you find, contract, and/or buy the property. When you find and contract a house worth $380,000 today for $310,000 from a motivated seller, then you have a locked-in profit of $70,000 (i.e., $380,000 – $310,000 = $70,000). You can sell it or keep it and hope it appreciates in value even more. Some skeptics say you can't find houses for 15 to 30 percent below what they are worth today. They are right—*they* can't because they are skeptical. Those who go out and search do find great deals. Hundreds of my students are finding them all of the time in all types of markets. It just takes time, persistent effort, and know-how. That's why you're reading this book.

your own community was selling for 15 years ago compared with now . . . and imagine what it will sell for 15 years from now. Of course, sometimes real estate goes down, or depreciates, but over time it generally appreciates in value if you buy it at *15 to 30* percent below what it's worth today. This should protect you from a down market in most cases. Besides, if you don't want to be tied down in a market, you can wholesale and lease-option real estate and avoid most of the risk of owning while still making a profit.

Any time is a good time to get into real estate because it's always been effective, producing results that can lead to great wealth.

Real Estate Investing Comes with Tax Advantages

If you buy a stock, make a profit, and sell that stock, you'll likely pay a capital gains tax on that profit. People say, "I don't want to do this real estate deal because if I sell the property, I'm going to make a lot of money and pay a lot in taxes, so I'm not going to do real estate." I have a different point of view.

One of my goals is to write the IRS a check for $5 million. I love to pay taxes because if I pay $5 million, that means I made $12 million and get to keep $7 million. If I send the IRS $100,000, that means I made $300,000 and kept $200,000. Real estate carries some distinct tax advantages (which are discussed in Chapter 3, "Wholesaling and Flipping"). In many cases, you can sell real estate without paying any taxes. You can buy and sell in a self-directed individual retirement account (IRA) or do a 1031 tax-free exchange if conditions permit.

Operate as a Business

You've just started a business investing in real estate. You're driving your car to look for properties, talking on the phone, and maybe taking trips related to your business. All of that adds up to expenses that can be taken as tax write-offs on your income tax return.

I recommend that you check with a knowledgeable accountant about write-offs in your situation. Owning and operating a business comes with specific tax advantages. For example, now that you're actively trying to make a profit in real estate, you can buy a computer and a copy machine for your business (plus phones, business-related gasoline for your car, etc.) and write off some or all of these expenses.

Do you like having gifts from the government? Suppose you make a good start in real estate and study all of these materials and then say, "I see how to make money in real estate; I understand all the credit finance techniques. But it's not for me. I don't want to make all that money." Congratulations, you're still going to make an incredible return on the time you invest learning about real estate investing, because if you buy your own home for even 15 percent below what it's worth—say you get

Robert's Tip

For the last 10 years, I've owned my own homes and moved every two years. Do I think it's exciting to pack everything I own, hold a garage sale, then go to garage sales in a new city to buy more stuff that I'll sell at a garage sale two years from now? No, but I move almost every two years because it's tax-free money.

a $500,000 home for $450,000—five years from now, you might be able to sell it for $700,000 and make $250,000 profit. How much tax would you likely pay on the sale of that house if it's your own home and you're married? Zero. That's because if you're married, you get a $500,000 exemption if you've owned the home for two years. In addition, you can get that exemption every two years. So every two years, you can buy your own home, sell it, make a lot of money, and likely pay no taxes.

Rental Property or Investment Property

Say you've had a small apartment building or 10 houses worth $300,000 each for 15 years that you bought for $3 million. About 15 years later, the worth doubled and you can make $3 million if you sell. You'd have to pay capital gains tax—about 20 percent depending on your tax bracket—on your $3 million in profit. That adds up to

The Best Real Estate Tax Deal for You

You can make up to $250,000 in tax-free profit on the sale of your own home if you are single, and you can make $500,000 if you are married and file jointly. However, you must live in the house for at least two of the past five years as your principal residence. Every two years or so, you can do the best tax-free real estate deal going.

Suppose you bought your house three years ago for $300,000 and now you sell it for $500,000. Your profit would be $200,000 because you bought it at the right price and it appreciated. That $200,000 is tax-free money to you. You can now find another good deal, live in that house for two years, and make more tax-free money when you sell it!

$600,000 in taxes, and you may have to recapture and pay taxes on some or all of the depreciation you took.

It's worthwhile getting information so you don't have to pay that, including finding out about doing a 1031 tax-free exchange. This tax exemption is available for investment property owners when you sell a property and buy a similar one for more than the amount of the first one. (The sale must take place within a certain time period.) Be sure to work with a qualified tax advisor who knows all the rules and regulations in your state. Chances are, you'll pay zero in taxes again.

Steps to Tax-Free Earnings

Your Own Home

- Bought in 1997 for $300,000
- Retail value of $370,000
- Sold in 2003 for $570,000
- You make $570,000 − $300,000 = $270,000 tax-free profit (if you qualify)

Investment Property Using 1031 Exchange

- First investment $40,000 in 1990
- Tax-free exchange—sold for $80,000 in 1994
- Found house worth $100,000, bought it for $80,000 in 1994
- Sold house for $100,000 in 1996
- Did a 1031 tax-free exchange for a house worth $150,000, bought for $100,000
- Sold house for $250,000 cash in 1999
- Used cash as a down payment on an apartment building worth $1 million, doing a 1031 tax-free exchange; owner has not paid any taxes on these properties

Example of 1031 Exchanges

One of my students bought a tiny house for $40,000 about 10 years ago, sold it for $80,000, and exchanged it into a $100,000 house. She found this $100,000 house for $80,000, then exchanged it for a $150,000 house that she purchased for $100,000. Now she's investing in apartment buildings that cost more than $1 million. She had paid zero in taxes because she kept exchanging, exchanging, and exchanging. With documentation in hand, she went to the bank or mortgage company and asked, "This apartment building is worth $1 million; would you lend us $700,000?" She borrows the funds and, again, pays zero in taxes, because, in general, borrowed funds are not taxed.

How I Got Started by Accident

Ten years ago, I had no desire to have a career in real estate. I was employed with a top financial consulting firm at the time. Then one day I met an older guy in Nashville, Tennessee. He was in his late sixties and he'd started buying little houses without using any of his own money. He would fix them up and rent them out. He had a junky old office, drove a beat-up old pickup truck, and dressed in torn overalls. Both he and his wife were lovely people but I almost walked out that day because I thought he had no money and wouldn't meet the financial requirements for working with our investment firm.

When I asked what he and his wife did for a living, he opened his old accounting book and said, "I've got about 120 houses paid for. I make about $60,000 a month and I take six months' vacation a year." He then asked me, "Robert, tell me, how's your job?"

At that time, I thought my job was pretty good. Yet even though the company handbook said we were supposed to have three weeks of vacation, those who took even one week of vacation were fired. That's when I suddenly realized that if *this* guy can make such good money in real estate investing, maybe I could, too.

This gentleman who got me started didn't understand wholesaling or lease optioning; over the previous 20 years, he had learned about buying and renting and buying fixer-uppers to sell—only a few of the many tools available to investors. Yet I could quickly calculate that owning 120 paid-for houses in my city (or any city, for that matter) meant that he was worth somewhere between $8 million and $15 million. I quickly realized I was speaking with a very wealthy man.

So I took the plunge. I interviewed other investors and thought maybe if I could do 20 percent as well as they did, I would be okay. For one whole year, I looked around, made plans, read a lot, talked to people, and looked at hundreds of houses. I made no money in the first year—I was still thinking about it, planning to do something, and I was stressed out and worried. Then I finally bought a duplex. I put it under contract and, because I didn't have any money or credit at the time, borrowed all the money for it. Ironically, I couldn't find the house I had just purchased! I closed on the house on a Tuesday afternoon and spent Wednesday, Thursday, and Friday driving around. I still couldn't find it. I can't read maps. I have no sense of direction. Finally I called the broker and said, "Could you please show me the property I just bought?"

That was the beginning. I started with a single duplex, then 5 duplexes, then 12 duplexes, and I quit my job about a year after my first purchase. I had $300 a month net coming in on each duplex I bought—$3,600 a month tax-free because, with my own business in real estate and owning rental property, I had many tax deductions, as you will. I was 29 years old and making $3,600 a month tax-free, and I had very little to do. I traveled, worked out, and went out a lot.

Then I decided if that approach works for 12 duplexes, I wanted to own 20 or more. I actually purchased about 200 properties. After three years, I learned how to wholesale, how to lease option, how to fix up and sell. When it's all added up, I've been involved in about 750 real estate transactions over the last decade.

THINK ABOUT IT

Some people spend most of their time thinking about what they *can't* do or what won't work. Some people, perhaps you, think about how they *can* do something. In my early years of investing, most people told me I couldn't buy any property or own my first duplex because I had no credit. Instead of listening to them, I found a cosigner who had great credit to partner with. I found the deals and my cosigner signed the loans with me so I could borrow the money I needed. Word of caution: Make sure you've found a *good deal* before you commit your credit or especially someone else's credit to a real estate deal. What have you accomplished in the past that people told you that you could not? How did it feel when you accomplished it?

12 Ways to Get Property without Using Your Own Money

There are various ways to acquire property even if you have no money.

1. Partner with People

Find people who have what you don't have—a lot of money and a lot of credit and very large cushions. Draw up a business plan that says, for example, together we're going to buy 100 houses over the next five years. You have the energy and the expertise to find good deals and

A Shining Example

Hugh is a 23-year-old, bright, ambitious young man. He read my books, bought my home study course, and attended a workshop that I give a couple of times a year. In the courses, I talk about finding money to invest in properties that doesn't come from banks or mortgage companies. As a matter of fact, Hugh, like many people, was having trouble getting good loans from banks or mortgage companies. Instead of quitting or letting his attitude turn negative, he used the techniques in this book to raise money from private individuals. In less than six weeks, he gained access to more than $1.2 million in cash from private lenders. Way to go, Hugh!

Follow in Hugh's footsteps and attend an upcoming seminar with Robert Shemin to learn about real estate investing. Call 888-302-8018 to get the full details.

manage them, and your partner might be a busy doctor, a lawyer, an accountant, or a retired executive who has a lot of money but is making only 3 to 5 percent return in decent years on his or her investments. These professionals would like to make 11 or 12 percent and reap some tax advantages and appreciation to bring their actual return to 15, 20, or 30 percent. However, don't tell them that because it could scare them. When you start promising people returns of more than 15 percent, they get nervous.

Draw up a plan to buy a house that's worth $200,000, which you can get for $180,000. Your partner goes down to the bank and signs a few papers. The bank loves to lend money to people with good credit who have secure jobs and a financial cushion—unlike a lot of self-employed people like us. So have your partner borrow the funds to purchase the house. Whose name is on the title of the house? Your partner's name or the name of your corporation or trust. Together, you determine what percentage of the house you each own: 50-50, 70-30, or whatever you agree on. Agree that you make all the decisions about renting and managing and making repairs, while your partner's name is on the loan papers.

Your partner would get some tax advantages for being in rental real estate—up to $25,000 a year write-off for the depreciation against regular income. (Do consult with your accountant and your partner's accountant to find out all of the advantages.) As the managing partner, you get all the control.

Five years down the road, if a house needs major repairs, your financially strong, deep-pocketed partner borrows another $10,000 (or takes another $10,000 out of a bank account or retirement or savings) to fix up the house. Then, another 10 years down the road, properties that were worth $20 million are now worth $28 million because property value has gone up and the debt has gone down—from $18 million to $15 million. You sell the houses you bought together and split the profits according to the percentage arrangement you made earlier. All the debt is paid off and your financial partner does well. You're both happy and you're both better off. Your partner has the money, and you have the expertise, time, and energy.

I know of at least 20 investors in the United States who own more than 200 properties, and their names are not on one bank loan or deed. They have zero liability for lawsuits because they have zero liability on the debt. They have recruited strong, informed partners who have clear written agreements and who understand that there might be a bad month or two. Partnering is one of the best ways to buy property, so find a good financial partner.

2. Wholesale Properties

This is when you find a property, put it under contract, wholesale it, flip it, get paid for finding good deals, and don't use any of your own money.

Let's take that a step further. If you definitely want to own property, why not wholesale or flip properties until you have enough cash to buy them? People love to spend their money to start to make money. Here's a radical concept: Let your revenues lead your expenses. If you want to get an office for $3,000, make $8,000 and then spend the $3,000. If you want to buy a $50,000 house, make $75,000 and buy the house for $50,000. If you want to buy a car for $20,000, flip five properties and pay cash for the car. If you want to buy five houses, find ten good deals, flip five, and buy five with the money you made wholesaling to put down payments on them. You can actually wholesale or work your way into owning property. That's one of the best ways to use other people's money. (See Chapter 3.)

3. Lease-Option Properties

Instead of borrowing money, lease the property with an option to buy. (See Chapter 4, "Lease Optioning.") For some reason, everyone wants to borrow money, get a 20- or 30-year loan, and be on the hook for the debt when they could lease-option it. If you borrowed the $100,000 to buy a house and everything changes in three years, or you simply don't like it—you want to move to another state, you win the lottery, you want to retire—then you're in debt for 20 or 30 years and could be

SECRETS OF BUYING AND SELLING REAL ESTATE

forced to sell it when it's not the best time to sell. But if you lease-option it, you can simply give the property back to the owner.

You have the *option* to buy it, not the *obligation,* and you can give it back, just as you do when you lease-option a car. In three years, if you want another car, instead of having to sell the lease-optioned car to pay off your debt, you just give it back. If it's not scratched up and if you haven't driven too many miles, you don't owe any more money. Now you can buy the new model that you didn't even know existed when you lease-optioned. Why obligate yourself to things that have no flexibility?

4. Owner's Terms

The other way people buy cars or houses is by borrowing the money from a bank, a finance company, or a leasing company. And they're tough. They make you fill out all these papers; they check your credit; your "round peg" has to fit exactly right in their "square hole." Sometimes it's difficult because maybe you had some pitfalls in life, or you didn't plan ahead, or you didn't keep financial controls well enough and your credit is not perfect. Maybe you can't borrow the money, or maybe you can borrow it but only at a high interest rate. Through a lease option, the seller becomes your bank. (See Chapter 4, "Ways to Source Funds" for details on how to work with owner's terms.)

5. Sell Some Assets

You can always generate cash by selling $10,000 to $150,000 of your assets (though you're probably looking for more creative ways). (See Chapter 4 for details on how to work with owner's terms.)

16

6. Should You Borrow from Credit Cards?

If someone says you need $20,000 down on a house to buy it and you don't have $20,000, where do you get it? Borrow—from equity lines, relatives, friends, enemies. If you borrow the down payment, none of your own money is in the property.

There's another source that I'm not recommending but that a lot of investors have used successfully: credit cards. At one time, I had over $180,000 of debt available on my credit cards, and the interest rate on most of them was 7 or 8 percent—those first six-months or one-year introductory rates. However, a rational economic person borrows as much as he or she can at the lowest rate interest for as long as possible. If you can find these deals and make 20 percent on your money or an infinite return on your money, what would you, as a rational decision maker, do?

Why Don't People Borrow Money?

One reason is they don't have a system to use it efficiently and control it. Underline the word *control*. Every Friday, you want to know what's coming in and what's going out, in both your business life and your personal life. Doing that will save you a massive headache, a nightmare, because one of the major reasons most businesses go under is lack of controls. Of course, that would never happen to you or little companies like Enron, MCI, airline companies, correct? Isn't that amazing? Billion-dollar companies all of a sudden say, "Last year we didn't make $8 billion; we lost $3 million. Somebody made a mistake." Doesn't that make you feel better about not being able to balance your bank account? Control your cash flow, and every Friday look at what came in and what went out.

7. Trade Services

Let's say someone needs $5,000 cash down and you don't want to pay that (because you're reading this book about how to buy property without using your own money). You could trade services for that down payment. I'm not kidding. I've had students baby-sit, wash cars, paint, repair computers, do yard work, consult—whatever they could do. They'd trade their services for a down payment. It's another way to be creative with money.

8. Find Something in the Property to Sell

This is one of my favorite ways to buy property without using your own money.

Let's say you found a good deal on a house that has an extra lot. You have a contract to control the house and lot, and you're going to close on it in 90 or 120 days (according to the contracts that you've learned how to negotiate in Chapter 7, "Negotiating Deals and Making Offers"). During that 90-day period, you find a buyer for the lot. The seller wants $10,000 down, you sell the lot for $12,000, and you do a simultaneous closing. The buyer shows up with $12,000 to buy the lot, the lawyer sells the lot, takes the money, and puts it down on the property.

Let me give you another example. A man I know had no cash and no credit, but he found a good deal on 2,000 acres. However, to buy it he needed a $100,000 down payment. Would you put a property under contract when the sellers want $100,000 and you have about $22 in the bank? Knowledge is power, and he knew about timber rights. He sold the timber rights for $175,000, which took about 45 days. That way, he got the $175,000, put $75,000 in his pocket, and used the rest for the down payment on the land. Then he started selling pieces of the land.

Let me tell you the two best businesses in the world: Buy whiskey by the bottle and sell it by the shot; buy land by the acre and sell it by the lot. In Las Vegas, they've figured out the first one very well. They buy a bottle of whiskey for $12 and sell you a shot for $4. There are 30 shots in a bottle. Similarly, you can buy a big chunk of land for $100,000 and carve out lots worth perhaps $20,000 each. Maybe there are 20 lots on that land. You divide up the property, sell the lots, then use those funds to buy more property without using your own money.

I'm from the South, and in Tennessee and Kentucky, a lot of land has valuable woods that people like to use for carving. I've had students take this information, buy five acres, sell the rights to get this rare wood, and then make tens of thousands of dollars and use that as their down payment. I've had people buy land with ginseng or other herbs. Please understand

How Do You Sell Something You Don't Own?

You've analyzed the property, done your research, talked to people, and have a lot of information. This land is valuable; it's worth more because it has something valuable on it like timber rights or ginseng. You know you can subdivide it and sell it. You did your research; you have a signed contract; you control the property. Now write another contract saying, "Contingent upon my being able to pass good title (as you learned in the section on contracts), you will buy the timber rights for $100,000 and we'll close in the next 90 days." You hand it all to the attorney, and the attorney arranges the simultaneous closings. (See more details about contracts in Chapter 8, "Dealing with Contracts.")

that marijuana is illegal; don't buy property with the idea of selling something illegal. Think about the other assets in that land that you can sell.

You control the property or option the property through contracts. "I option to buy your property for $10,000 down and, for the rest, owner's terms." Then you have the option to buy it, and that's when you sell the timber rights, the land, the old car that was left at a deceased person's home, the furniture remaining there, and so on.

9. Flip Multiple Properties

You already understand wholesaling. It is one of the best ways to make money in real estate without using your own money. Even better is flipping multiple properties. Instead of flipping a single house, you can flip five at a time. Say you find an old landlord or landlady who has five houses and will sell you all five, but wants $10,000 down on each. That's $50,000. You put all five under contract for 100 days or 90 days and you flip two of them to someone else for cash using our wholesaling methods.

Let's say two of the houses are worth $300,000 and you've got them under contract for $220,000. You flip each of them for $260,000, making $40,000 profit on each of the houses. You go to a simultaneous closing, the lawyer sells the houses, and you make an $80,000 profit at the closing table. The lawyer uses $50,000 of that $80,000 for your down payment on all five homes.

10. Create a Note and Sell It

This is an advanced technique for buying property without your own money.

Say you find a seller who wants to sell a house. It's worth $300,000 but the seller needs $220,000 cash. You don't have the $220,000 cash; you can't borrow it; you've done all the negotiating you can; the seller's bottom line is $220,000 cash. You can get the cash by creating a note and selling it. (In Chapter 11, "Borrowing When You Have Bad Credit," you'll learn how to broker notes, which is basically what you're doing, but now you're brokering your own note.)

Work with your note buyers to structure the deal. They'll tell you the numbers to put in, the interest rate and the term, to net out the $220,000 cash. Say you write a note for $280,000 at 10 percent interest for 20 years. Depending on the credit rating and market conditions, you might find a note buyer who would purchase that note for $220,000. He or she would be buying it at a discount. The seller gets the cash. However, in this example, that wouldn't be a good deal because you borrowed $280,000 on a $300,000 house; even so, it is a way to control the property without using your own money. Create a note, sell the note. You can sell all of the note or part of the note to get the cash the seller needs. If the numbers are right, you could get into a good deal without using your own money.

11. Make Full-Price Offers

Would you like to be able to make full-price offers on houses in hot real estate markets and not use a penny of your own money? You can get more real estate by making full-price offers, which is the reverse of everything we've been talking about. Use none of your own money to buy these houses. This is a highly advanced technique. Very few people in the United States are doing it or know about it. It won't work every time, but it works some of the time.

This technique works only on houses or property with low mortgage balances. If the house is worth $500,000 and the mortgage is $400,000, it probably will not work. You need access to amortization schedules. They're available on my web site at Shemin.com, where you'll find a finance calculator and mortgage calculator. Work the amortizations to see what your payment will be, what the debt payment will be, and what the other property's payment will be.

Try a zero-interest loan, which is another way of saying *free money.* You could call this the "free money loan." You go to a rental-property owner who has a low- or no-mortgage balance on a house. Let's say it's $300,000 and the property will rent for at least $3,000 a month. You always want more coming in than going out, so do your homework. First, try to negotiate a lower price with the owners. However, they won't negotiate; it's worth $300,000 and they want $300,000.

Most investors would walk away from this deal but you have so many tools that you never have to walk away. Every time they say no, you just ask more questions and come up with another option. You'd say, "I'll pay you $300,000 in full. I'll pay you $1,000 a month for 300 months." What if they say no to that, even though $1,000 a month for 300 months is $300,000? They may say they need more money than that each month. You counter with, "I'll pay you $3,000 a month for 100 months." Some people just want the monthly income to pay off some debt, get out of the debt, move on—they want some cash.

Remind them that on investment property, if they take the whole $300,000 in cash, they have to pay taxes on the gain, unless they know about a 1031 tax-free exchange. If they sell the investment property they've had for 20 years for $300,000 and the base is zero (or the loan is paid off), they're probably going to pay 20 percent tax on it, or $60,000. I suggest always turning everything into a question. Ask, "How would you like to save $60,000 in taxes?"

In today's market, that's not a bad deal for the seller, because the seller who takes that $300,000 is going to pay tax on it. You take away $60,000, leaving only $240,000, which the seller can put in a mutual fund or CD. Because banks are paying 1 to 3 percent interest rates, your seller is not losing that much.

You need to understand real estate finance and present values. The present value of $300,000 today with no interest is pennies on the dollar. You are buying that house for about 30 to 40 cents on the dollar, or

A Way to Defer Taxes

A 1031 tax-free exchange is basically deferred tax, but it can end up being no tax at all. When you die, your estate gets the property at the marked-up value and there's no tax due, so basically you keep exchanging your way into oblivion until you die. On tax-free exchanges, you make money by borrowing to buy more expensive property. You buy it, and later you refinance it, pull your money out, put it in your pocket, and pay no taxes. But if you sell all your property before you die and don't do another 1031 exchange, then you must pay the tax based on the last property.

Anytime you can defer taxes for a year (or two or five), think about how much money you're saving because you can use those funds to make money. Would you rather have $30,000 in your pocket or in the IRS's pocket? This year, next year, or the next? Most investors sell their property, pay taxes, wait a month to buy another one, sell that property, and pay taxes on that one. If they had exchanged it, they would have had much more money in their pocket to put to use.

approximately $120,000 in today's money. The most powerful wonder of the world is the time value of money. Would you rather have $1,000 today or 50 years ago? Consider that $300,000 in 300 months from now is only about $100,000 today. So you are really buying the house for $100,000.

If you get nothing else from this book, learn this concept. Have the paperwork drawn up so you can just fill in the blanks, and go around to 200 potential sellers who have low mortgage balances, and you could probably get some deals. If you do nothing but focus on this one creative finance technique for 10 hours a week during the next six months, you will probably find one deal. What if it is just your own home? If it is only one house for $200,000, five years from now you would probably make well over $100,000 in net worth equity.

Make sure the sellers understand what they're doing. Have the closing attorney do an amortization schedule, because if there's debt on the property, *your* debt may go down faster than *their* debt. In 10 years, if they had a big debt on the property, and if you've paid down all your debt to zero and they still have $50,000 debt and you're ready to sell it or refinance it, they'd have to come to closing with cash. The sellers and you both need to understand that this doesn't work for property with high debt on it. So run the amortization schedules. Have your mortgage banker, your attorney, or yourself get on the Internet and confirm that their debt, if any, is going to go down as your debt is going down.

You're not going to trick people or hide it; if this solution meets their needs, they may go for it. Show them how much money they're saving on taxes. They're probably better off. Because of the opportunity cost of money, they're only going to get 3 or 4 percent return on their money.

People don't generally make 20 percent on their money the way they did that year when tech stocks went through the roof. Again, they don't have $300,000 to invest; they have only $240,000 after taxes, so it isn't as bad for them as it sounds and if it meets their needs, you might want to go for it.

At some point when the property is paid down, it would be sold for a big profit. This is very important: In our business, when do we always prefer

---

What about Taxes on a Full-Price Offer?

If you make a full-price offer on a house and it's accepted, how much do the sellers have to pay in taxes? If the sellers have lived in the house for the previous two years and it qualifies for the exemption (i.e., you can sell your own home and make up to $250,000 tax-free profit if you're single or $500,000 tax-free profit if you're married), they will probably not pay taxes. If it's an investment property and it's been less than a year, they have to pay their income tax plus the self-employment tax. If they've had it more than a year with the intention of holding it, then they're going to pay capital gains tax, which right now is about 20 percent. If they do a 1031 tax-free exchange, they may not have to pay any tax if they structure the transaction properly.

If they do an installment sale, which is 0 percent financing (at $200,000, you pay them $1,000 for 200 months), they pay tax only as they get the cash, so you've drawn out their tax bill. Instead of paying it this year, you've elongated it to the length of the payment cycle. How much tax they pay also depends on their tax basis in the property. Understand the fundamentals with owner's terms installment sales. Ask what their tax basis is, how much tax they would have to pay, and whether they would like to avoid paying all that this year by spreading it out. Explain how that's basically paying less because of the time value of money.

---

to make a profit? *Today.* We don't want to delay profits for 5 or 20 years. Everything we do must be profitable today.

It's hard to find property, especially in the higher end, that you purchase for full price and rent out for more. There is a curve. A $100,000 house might rent for $1,200. A $150,000 house might rent for $1,600. A $200,000 house might rent for $2,000. But an $800,000 house isn't going to rent for $8,000, or eight times what the $100,000 rented for. There's a curve. If it's structured right, you make a profit every month.

When the debt is paid down, or as it's being paid down, you can sell it. The way you make a big profit is to sell it. And when you sell a property you never want to do owner's terms—you always want cash. You could refinance it and pay down the $300,000 to $150,000. You could go to the bank and borrow $200,000 or $250,000.

When do you make money in real estate, really? You may make a little bit of money each month when you rent it. You may have tax advantages, depreciations, appreciation, but that's equity. You *really* make money in real estate when you sell it or refinance it. Therefore, sell your property quickly. Flip it. Wholesale everything. Why delay the selling? Why delay making the profit?

It can also be advantageous to hold property and build up net worth for the long term, depending on your plan, your needs, your desires. You should refinance your property all the time, because you want your money to work for you. I usually refinance mine every three years. When your money is sitting in equity it's building up, and if your goal is equity buildup and you don't need that money to live on today, this approach might fit your plan.

Most people sacrifice, struggle, and struggle some more to build up a nice net worth, and when they die, their children are very happy. My neighbor's mother's husband bought real estate for 30 years: bought it, fought with the tenants, struggled, bought property, and bought more property. Every evening they'd fight at the dinner table. She'd be yelling, "Why do you have this property? It's driving you crazy; it's stressing you out; we don't have any free time; we can't travel; you're dealing with the tenants, the property. I hate you, I hate real estate, I hate rental property, I hate your tenants." It was a big problem for 20 or 30 years. Then he died. Now every day his wife says she loves real estate. She sold all the properties and took the profit.

Think about where the profit is, where the money is, and when you are going to take it. Consider two ways to take it: selling or refinancing.

12. Borrow All the Money

Notice that I didn't put borrowing as the first option; I put it as the last one. Who do you borrow the money from? Banks and mortgage companies. If you have good credit, these days you can get 100 percent loan to value—100 percent. You do an 80 percent first mortgage and a 20 percent second mortgage. If you don't have good credit, you can find someone with good credit for a partner, but the deal has to be good enough so the numbers work.

You may want to buy property, but you have bad credit. Even if your credit is bad, if you are buying your own home and possibly even investment property, a mortgage company may still give you a loan—but at a much lower loan to value. Let's say the house is worth $100,000. If your credit is good or perfect, a mortgage company might lend you $90,000, $95,000, or $100,000—in other words, 90, 95, or 100 percent loan to value. Those kinds of loans are available now. If you know the people at your local bank, they, too, may offer you favorable terms.

All federally chartered banks have to lend money in low- to moderate-income neighborhoods because of the Community Reinvestment Act (CRA). See if any of your loans fall under CRA rules, and you may receive better terms—or at least loans—because you're rehabilitating properties in low- to moderate-income neighborhoods. Also, if you are a woman, a minority, or someone who is helping low- to moderate-income people, you may want to call the Small Business Administration and your local chamber of commerce to see if they have any special loans or grants available to help you start your own business.

CHAPTER 2

The greatest things in the world have been done by those who systematized their work and organized their time.
—ORISON SWETT MARDEN

Systems for Success

One thing that gets in the way of success as a real estate investor is what I call "being in our own way." We think too much; we worry too much. That's why we need systems for our real estate investment business.

You might fret, "Oh, no, a tenant called and can't pay the rent this month. What do I do?" Then you spend the next week stressing out, not taking any action. But if your policy says, "The rent is due on the first of the month; it's late on the eleventh; we evict on the fifteenth or work out a payment plan in writing," you have no decisions to make.

By having a system, you reduce the amount of time you spend thinking and worrying. Some people go to their jobs every day at 8:00 A.M., make 10 phone calls from 8:00 to 9:00, and fill in 10 reports from 10:00 to 11:00. They know what they have to do—their company and every job has a system. You, too, can set up a "don't worry" system for your business of buying real estate without using your own capital or credit.

At McDonald's, the employees have a policy and procedures manual that lays out practically every detail: "Open bun, put burger on bun, put pickle on burger, close bun." Consequently, these employees have very few decisions to make. You can copy this model by writing a policy and procedures manual that frees you from making dozens of decisions every day.

Robert's Tip

To drastically change your life and your profitability, create a ritual: Take 30 minutes every Friday and review how you actually spent your time during the week. Record all of your activities and how long they took, and write down which activities made money for you. One week, for example, I had 82 meetings, was on the phone for 30 hours, and shopped for drywall for 4 hours at a store.

I estimate that most of us spend 70 to 80 percent of our time on activities that make absolutely no money and don't really help us. And yet we're busy and excited and stressed out. Take 30 minutes every Friday and review what you did the week before, then focus on spending your time on more profitable activities. If you do this, I predict you will drastically increase your productivity, your happiness, and your profitability. When I started doing that a few years ago, it changed how I did everything. I got rid of some businesses so I could focus on what was more fun and more profitable—and you need to do the same.

As real estate investors, it's critical to build systems for success. Everything should be a system. Even getting properties without using your own money. When you call the bank and can't make a payment, the bank representatives don't say, "Oh my God, what do we do? Let's have meetings; let's worry about it. He said he lost his job and she said she's not feeling well. They're really nice, what do we do?" Instead of making up solutions as they go along, they follow their procedures.

You don't have to make it up anymore; just develop and follow your own system and procedures, recording them in a policy and procedures manual. All successful businesses have a system. Set it up, operate it, and fine-tune your real estate investing like any successful business.

System #1: Focus on Profit

You may have thoughts like this: "I'm busy all week, and I know I'm really working hard, but I'm not making any money."

Or you may find an activity that is extremely lucrative for you. For instance, one year I wholesale-flipped more than 50 properties while doing other activities, including running a property management business. That kept me extremely busy . . . and stressed out. I had employees, an office, a lot of activity, a lot of stress. Money came in and money went out. But that management business made zero profit. I was focusing on being busy and doing things I was good at because I knew I was a good property manager. Chances are, you're good at many things, but you must focus on what you're *best* at—what makes your business profitable.

Daily Log Worksheet

Track your activities and the time spent on them every day. Include your best estimate of your enjoyment and profitability for each activity.

	Activity	Time Spent	Enjoyment Factor (1–10, with 10 being most)	Profitability Factor (1–10, with 10 being highest)
1.				
2.				
3.				
4.				
5.				
6.				
7.				
8.				
9.				
10.				

System #2: Find Good Deals and Motivated Sellers

Focus on finding deals, because almost everything else you do in real estate is a waste of your precious time. Some of the activities—the paperwork, the repairs, the meetings with contractors, the property management—are necessary, but they're not moneymaking activities.

If you find a deal that's worth $600,000 for $400,000, you have several options to choose from: Do a lease option, flip it, fix it and sell it, rent it to make monthly income, and so on. What's most profitable is finding that deal. It may surprise you to know I've found a lot of deals spending only two to four hours a week looking. I have spent 20 to 30 hours looking for deals, making a ridiculous amount of money that would be unfit to print. But over time, I shifted from focusing on activities that kept me busy and stressed out to focusing on finding deals.

Finding a good deal in real estate is a numbers game. You have to look at a bunch of properties and talk to a lot of people to find a good or even great deal. Most successful investors use only one or two or three ways to find good deals. But I'm going to show you dozens of ways to find them.

A good deal in real estate can be defined as a sale price of a *minimum* of 20 percent below what that property is worth in the retail market today, taking into account the cost of repairs. If a house is worth $100,000, and I can get it for $80,000 (which is a 20 percent discount) but it needs $20,000 worth of repairs, then it's not a good deal. If the $100,000 house can be purchased and repaired for $75,000, that's 75 cents on the dollar, or a 25 percent margin. In today's tight, competitive real estate market, a lot of deals are what I call "20 percenters," which are priced at least 20 percent below what they're worth. It's important to have a good-sized margin, because you could face more repairs than expected, or you could incur holding costs if it takes a long time to sell.

A good deal in real estate means you've found a motivated seller (see Chapter 5, "Avenues Leading to Motivated Sellers," for more about how to find eager sellers). Again and again, ask the question, "Why are you

---

Robert's Tip

Why would people sell a property for less than it's worth? Because they find themselves in a tough situation. Or sometimes people simply do things that don't make sense. Why don't they wear their seat belts? Why don't they go to the gym? Why do they smoke cigarettes? Why do they drink too much? Don't waste time and energy trying to understand why.

---

selling?" You waste your time trying to force a deal if the seller isn't pressured to sell because of a divorce, ill health, pending foreclosure, or whatever. Make it a win-win situation.

Let's say you could find a property worth $80,000 and pay $60,000. In southern California, we'd have to add some zeros, so let's say you bought a house worth $800,000 for $600,000.

To get those prices and make it worthwhile to buy as an investment, that property must have a motivated seller. Who are motivated sellers? People going through a divorce, having an estate sale, dealing with a foreclosure, being transferred out of state, and so on. Maybe they're older people who have to sell their home because it needs repairs and they don't want to do them.

Would lenders give you $600,000 to purchase a property worth $800,000? Probably. But if you can't get a loan from the bank, you can turn to a real estate partner with good credit or lots of money or to a hard moneylender or to another investor to lend you the funds. You could borrow the funds or maybe do owner's terms (i.e., the owner lends you the money so he or she can sell the property quickly). (By the

THINK ABOUT IT

Rodney, a student of mine, found a one-bedroom penthouse condominium on the ocean in South Beach, Miami, Florida, through a real estate agent. The condo was incredible. It was listed for about $510,000, the fully appraised value. Rodney asked the realtor why the seller was selling. She replied that the owner had six homes: one in Italy, one in New York, and several others around the world. He had not visited his condo in South Beach for more than two years and simply didn't want it any more. Rodney negotiated and got the condo under contract for $430,000, with its expensive furniture included. He wholesaled, or flipped, the condo to another person within three weeks for $485,000, or $30,000 below its worth. Rodney made about $45,000 profit on this deal. He didn't buy it; he didn't use or borrow any money. Instead, he got paid for finding a good deal and making everyone happy. Why did the seller accept an offer for about $80,000 less than the condo was worth? Because he wanted to. He was so wealthy, it would be like throwing out some old shoes! Don't worry about his reasons; it doesn't make any difference. Just do it.

I suggest that you stop trying to figure out why people do the things they do. Focus instead on your own activity. Worry only about what you're doing. That will be enough to keep you busy.

way, if that owner doesn't use a 1031 tax-free exchange and resells for $600,000 the same property purchased 20 years ago for $100,000, he would pay $120,000 in taxes—almost 20 percent of that $600,000.)

Knowledge is power. Just by knowing that 1031 tax-free exchanges exist, you could help someone who qualifies save more than $100,000 in taxes. Perhaps you could work with a local accountant or real estate closing attorney who does 1031 exchanges and advertise for people who want to sell their investment properties without paying any capital gains taxes.

You can begin to see that there are ways to purchase property without using any of your own funds if you find the property to be a good enough value. Even if you don't have a lot of cash or great credit, if you find a property that's selling for 20 to 30 percent below its worth, someone will step in and either lend you the money or pay you for finding this good deal.

To find willing sellers, you could run ads and distribute flyers that say something like this: "Sell your property and pay zero taxes. Find out if you qualify. Call 888-302-8018." Be sure to review Chapter 5, "Avenues Leading to Motivated Sellers," for lots of techniques.

Willing to Sell for a Dollar

A few years ago, I answered a House for Sale ad and asked the seller, "Why are you selling?" He said, "I'm getting divorced and I've got to sell our house." This executive home outside of Nashville sat on five acres and was worth at least $550,000. I asked, "What would you like for the house without negotiating? I don't like to negotiate and you probably don't want to, either. What would be the least you'd take for this house?" He said, "Well, I'd like to get $1 for it." I laughed and asked again. He replied, "I want $1. Really. The judge has ordered me to sell the house and split the proceeds with my ex-wife. I can't wait to give her 50 cents." So I put in an offer for $1 on the house. The judge rejected the offer, but eventually I did buy the house for a lot less than it was worth.

System #3: Find Good Buyers

Once you find good deals, you need to find good buyers. People often ask about my system for finding buyers, and I tell them it's very complicated. A few months ago, I sold 14 duplexes, a big investment for a potential investor. I found that investor by running an ad in the local newspaper. It cost me about $40 for one Sunday ad and generated about 30 calls from potential buyers. I screened them using the system explained in Chapter 4 and found several serious buyers. The fifth caller bought it, and I made a lot of money from that deal.

System #4: Build a Database

Capture the names of everyone you meet for your database. If you have a computer, use ACT or a similar type of contact management program. If you don't have a computer, just keep a folder and write down every

How Many Calls Do You Want to Make?

Professional telemarketers can make 40 to 60 calls in an hour if they're focused and really going. So get focused: Spend at least three hours a week making phone calls. You won't connect with everyone. You'll get voicemail and busy signals. Some people won't call you back—as in any business. But if you were to call for three focused hours a week and could call only 30 people in an hour, you'd still reach between 50 and 100 of them. Over six months, how many people would you call—and how many potential deals would you find?

person who is a potential buyer: name, address, phone number, fax number, and e-mail address. Also, record what type of property these people would like to buy so that when you find a deal, you can look through your list and fax, e-mail, or call them. Every real estate agent, every mortgage person, every investor, every landlord, every landlady, every person you contact from newspaper ads—add to your list. You're setting up a system for finding buyers.

Most people who do well financially have connections and keep making more. Everyone you speak with should be listed in your contact database under one of the following categories:

1. Sellers of properties
2. Buyers of properties
3. Financers of properties and potential partners in your real estate business

System #5: Find Sources of Money

If you're serious about real estate and finding deals, you'll run out of money and need to involve people who have money. That's why you'll need systems for finding people with money.

Build a strong network of mortgage brokers, bankers, wealthy people, investors, retired investors, and other people with money. As a fallback, you can always run an ad in the paper to source these people. (See Chapter 6, "Ways to Source Funds.")

System #6: Build in Leisure Time

Most likely, when you start out in a new business, particularly in real estate investing, you discover it's fun, exciting, and profitable. You may become addicted to it. When you run your own business, you start working 60-hour weeks, even 80-hour weeks. And all of a sudden, you're working all the time. Your personal life, your family life, and your spiritual life could begin to suffer.

The whole reason you started your business was to achieve financial freedom. But soon you'll find yourself, like I did, working all the time. Perhaps you will then qualify as a workaholic and join my new group— real estate anonymous (REA). "Hi, my name is Robert. I can't stop answering the phone, doing deals, working Sunday to Saturday and Wednesday night, because it's fun, it's profitable, it's exciting."

The following ideas will help you set up a system right now so you won't overdo it.

Set Office Hours

You'll add to your enjoyment if you set office hours. Decide, if this is a part-time business, "I'm going to work Wednesday from 4:00 to 7:00, diligently and with focus, and I'm going to work Saturday from 1:00 to 5:00 or Sunday from 11:00 to 4:00." You'll find that you focus better and accomplish more when you have a finite amount of time to work. If you gave yourself seven days a week to work, you'd probably spread out whatever work had to be accomplished over those seven days.

Whether you're a part-time or full-time investor, set your office hours and keep them.

Delegate

Every business has multiple components, especially running your own real estate investing. Find out what you like to do, what you're good at, then do those things yourself and hire others to do the things you don't like. Could you learn to change the brakes on your car? Change your oil? Even cut your own hair? You probably could figure out how to do these things, but you don't because you don't want to. It's stressful, it's a headache, you're not that good at it, and others are better equipped to do it than you, so you don't mind paying these specialists. Be careful when you get into real estate investing; you may try to do everything. "I'm going to paint, drywall, take out the garbage, do the bookkeeping and computer work, list the properties, write up all the papers, do the title searches, become an appraiser." The thought of doing all those jobs holds a lot of real estate investors back. Whatever tasks cause you headaches, simply hire other people to do them.

Robert's Tip

Do this experiment. Give yourself, your children, or a friend a task and insist it has to be done within one week. How long do people take to get things finished? You'll find it takes them a full week. Do you remember when you finally sat down to write your term paper in high school? Yes, the night before your paper needed to be turned in. You'll likely find that people tend to do a job at the last minute and take only as much time as they have. Try it yourself.

Robert's Tip

It actually took me 10 years to figure that I had to delegate out. In the beginning, I looked at the properties, analyzed them, did the paperwork, and managed them all myself. I was the subcontractor and general contractor, busy and stressed out all the time. Today, my job is to run the business. I let other people look for deals; I let title lawyers do the paperwork; I let bookkeepers do the bookkeeping; I let computer experts do the computer work; I let Realtors sell the property. Instead of doing everything myself, I manage everyone else's activities.

Find good people and delegate to them. That will reduce your headaches and increase your profit.

System #7: Earn Residual Income

I'm an attorney by training. About five years ago someone told me what I'm about to tell you. I was very skeptical.

Pre-Paid Legal Services, Inc.

A friend told me about a legal insurance company with lawyers all over the country. At that time, I was doing tons of real estate, and I signed up for this service to prove my friend wrong. The first case I had was one of the most complicated title problems I've ever encountered in my life.

I could not close on a property because of an old mechanic's lien on it. No one knew how to release it. I was told to hire an attorney, which normally would cost about $200 an hour. As a member of Pre-Paid

Legal Services, Inc., the visits were included in my fee of $26 a month. A competent attorney handled my case and cleared the title.

Of course there are different plans, rates, and coverages, so please consult my web sites for more details. Disclosure: I am *not* an employee of Pre-Paid Legal Services, Inc. I am an independent associate. Please visit www.prepaidlegal.com/go/shemin and www.prepaidlegal.com/info/shemin to find out more.

I'm convinced this is a necessary service, and it also provides income for me. I sign up most people by sending them to my web site. For example, if I'm on the phone with people in California, Texas, or New York, and they say they want to do Pre-Paid Legal, I send them to my site, where they watch a video about the service and, if they decide to participate, sign up for the service online.

Working with Pre-Paid Legal as I do, you get a lot of support, complete with online education. When you become an associate with us, we train you every week, and the training includes lots of conference calls. I ask everybody I talk to, "Have you done your will? Do you have legal questions? Check this web site. Pre-Paid Legal (www.pre-paidlegal.com) is good stuff. You'll be in good company. Some of our clients are Honeywell and Martin Marietta. They get it for all of their employees."

Here's the commission structure. Someone who tries out the membership sends in $26 plus a one-time $10 sign-up or application fee. If you also sign up as an associate, you'll be paid $75 for each new member you sign up. After you sell three memberships, you make $100 for each new member. If you want to make extra money every month, you could talk to 10 people at lunch. Of those, maybe five will sign up and you'll earn $500.

When we visit small companies and talk to 50 people, usually 30 to 40 in the group sign up for Pre-Paid Legal, which is $3,000. Once you've been trained to introduce and sell this service to groups, you could be earning that much money, too. Pre-Paid Legal has a commission structure similar to many large financial services and insurance companies in the world.

There are three ways to make money with Pre-Paid Legal. The first is to sell memberships. That's how I started. I'd sell one and make $100. I'd sell another and make another $100, and so on. The second way to make money is to sell many memberships at a time as a voluntary automatic deduction to people in small groups (e.g., associations, churches, employee groups, etc.). The third way is to have agents or associates working for you so you can make overrides from the memberships they sell. One month while I was out of the United States, my group sold 500 memberships. I made about $30 override from each of those sales, which totals $15,000. Of course, your results may vary. But this is certain: You won't make anything if you don't *do* anything.

The first year Pre-Paid Legal trained me how to do this business, I didn't listen to anyone and consequently made very little money. The second year, I realized another associate was making more than $1 million, so I decided to just follow his instructions. Using his system, I found out how well it works. A lot of people with less skill than I have are making more than $100,000 a year because they follow a simple system. You can learn more at www.pre-paidlegal.com/info/shemin or call 888-302-8018.

The biggest winner with Pre-Paid Legal is the member, who gets legal services affordably. The second biggest winners are the law firms;

Robert's Tip

Here's a way to get wealthy in life: Don't get involved in any business that doesn't have residual income. Stop trading your hours for dollars. If you don't go to work next month, you likely won't get paid. Pre-Paid Legal is a good example of residual income. You get paid today and next year and the year after that. I have met people who have not sold a Pre-Paid Legal membership in 10 years, yet every year they receive $200,000 in residual income. *Residual Income Creates Happiness = RICH.*

If you don't like to sell, sign up as an associate and recruit two or three go-getters who like to sell. Then, when they sell lots of Pre-Paid Legal memberships, you'll earn money on both the overrides and the residuals on those overrides.

---

they're making a lot of money. The third biggest winner is the salesperson who earns a commission on membership sales. The payments come in every day. Wouldn't you like getting paid every day?

In Western Europe, most people carry a legal plan. But in the United States, only 3 percent have one. Pre-Paid Legal is growing exponentially, so there's a lot of opportunity. This business isn't for everyone, but it may be for you. When you sign up to be an associate for a one-time fee of $149, you attend a training class in your area. At the four-hour training session, you'll learn all about commissions and how to sell memberships. It's very easy.

I continue to work in real estate, but Pre-Paid Legal is another great business that takes only two to eight hours a week. I see it as a moral obligation to help people with a service such as this. Everyone knows people with legal problems—wills, cars, credit, insurance, alimony, contractors, leases, money owed to them. Now you can help people and get paid for it. (Check out www.prepaidlegal.com/info/shemin.)

Residual Income Worksheet
Getting *RICH: Residual Income Creates Happiness*

Owning and investing in real estate, whether you use your own money or someone else's, can create wealth and residual income for you and your family. Fill out this worksheet to determine where you are today and where you will be in the future in regard to annual residual income you'll have to live on.

	Today	**10 years**	**20 years**	**30 years**
Assets				
Debts				
Net worth				
Residual income				
Real estate				
Business				
Retirement/ pensions				
Social Security				
Other investments				
Other				
Total				

Financially, where do *you* want to be in the future?

CHAPTER 3

He who draws only on his own resources easily comes to an end of his wealth.
—WILLIAM HAZLITT

Wholesaling and Flipping

One of the best ways for people to begin in real estate and to make money without using their own money is wholesaling properties, or flipping them.

Why wholesale? You could get into rehabbing, rentals, buying and holding property, but all of these have drawbacks. If you're rehabbing properties you never have enough money to buy the property, hold it, fix it, and wait to sell it. If you have rental property you have to buy it, fix it, manage it, put up with the tenants, and you won't have cash until you sell it or refinance it. Buying and holding requires borrowing money. The only time you make any serious money in real estate is when you sell or refinance. Why not skip the borrowing, fixing, and managing by wholesaling it? Get in and get out; flip them and make cash. Do that for six months or a year until you have a bunch of cash in your bank account. Then you can think about buying, holding, fixing, and renting.

Basically, *wholesaling* means getting paid for finding a good deal. Not owning it, not buying it, not taking title to it, not borrowing money, not dealing with contractors, not having really any liability if you structure your contracts right. You strictly get paid for finding good deals. How can you sell something or get paid for something you don't own? Well, just about everything in the world is flipped, or wholesaled.

For example, you go to a car dealership to buy a brand-new car. The salesperson conveniently offers you financing for that car, even though the dealership doesn't own it. It has a contract or an option with the car's manufacturer. If the dealership sells it to you for $40,000 and had a floor-plan agreement to pay the manufacturer $34,000, the dealership makes $6,000 (plus a potential bonus for selling several cars). The car dealership just "flipped" you a car.

The chair you're sitting on, the desk you work at, the couch you sit on at home, the television set you watch—just about everything you buy is wholesaled, or flipped. A friend of mine locates vacant lots for large retailers. He might, for example, visit a farmer who owns property on the edge of town and ask to put the land under contract for $100,000 with a contingency. His contingency clause usually says that the contract or option to buy is contingent on his partners' approval, his partners being the company to whom he is going to "wholesale" the property. Then he meets with the retail people and asks, "What would you pay for this land to put one of your big stores on?" They may be willing to pay $200,000, so he takes the company's $200,000 and gives the farmer (or the commercial broker who represents the farmer) $100,000. They close the deal and my friend, in effect, gets paid for finding the deal.

The farmer in this case was happy to receive $100,000. The company wanted the land to build a superstore, factory, or office and was happy to pay $200,000. My friend made $100,000 for finding the deal. He used a contract to buy it for $100,000. He had another contract to sell it to the company for $200,000. The attorney or title company took both contracts, closed the deal, and paid my friend $100,000 for putting a willing buyer and able seller together. He didn't spend or use his own money or credit.

Brainstorming Worksheet

What type of deals do you want to wholesale? _____

_____

_____

_____

What other types of goods, assets, or services could you wholesale?

_____

_____

_____

Components of Wholesaling

You can do a lot to increase your chances of success when wholesaling real estate. Become familiar with the following components.

Get Preapprovals for Funding

Never sign a contract with buyers until they're preapproved. Get a written verification that this transaction has been preapproved by a mortgage company or bank, or have the buyers show written proof that they have adequate funds available. By doing that, you can make sure the probability of deals falling through drops drastically.

According to a survey of more than 1,000 investors I conducted recently, over 40 percent of all contracts for sale fall through because the buyer could not get the cash or financing to close. You can avoid this by requiring confirmation, in writing, that your buyer has been preapproved or has the cash in hand.

THINK ABOUT IT

How many times have people told you they were going to do something, but didn't do it? It's frustrating, isn't it? That's why I suggest making it your business policy and procedure to put every agreement *in writing*. When lenders say they will lend you money, get their statements *in writing*. When other investors say they have the cash to do your deal, get proof *in writing*. When contractors say they'll fix something at a property by a certain date, get it *in writing*. When people say they'll pay you some money, get that promise *in writing*. Can you think back to an incident where this would have served you well? Make it a habit now.

Insist on an Inspection Clause

Insist on putting tight inspection clauses into your contracts. Here's an example of this: Say I want to buy a house from Mr. Motivated Seller who's moving out of the country. The house is worth $200,000 and he'll sell it to me for $100,000. It's the deal of the century, right? The contract I present requires an inspection and approval before closing. That means I can back out of the contract anytime before closing, subject to inspecting the property. The seller might protest and won't accept that condition. I reply, "It's a vacant home. What if kids break the windows? What if there's a fire or flood? What if something happens? Do you mean I've got to buy it even if the windows are broken and the walls are torn out? I insist on including that clause if I'm going to close on this property." If the seller still doesn't agree, I'm faced with a business decision: If it's a good enough deal, I might take the risk and close on it, despite the seller not agreeing to guarantee the house's condition. If I know I can sell it and make a profit, I go ahead.

Include a Clear Title Clause

Here's a good example to illustrate why it's important to get a clear title clause in the contract. You want to buy a house for $20,000. You have it under contract; it's a good deal. You're planning to rehab it and then sell it. Fixing it up will cost $5,000, so you'll have $25,000 in it and can sell it for $50,000 or $60,000. Your net would be $30,000—and that's a killer deal, right? But when you go to close on this deal, you find out the seller doesn't have clear title to the property and therefore can't pass it on. (Note: Always make sure that the seller has and can pass on a valid title. And always get a title insurance policy when you buy a property.)

What do you do? Start by talking to a decision maker at the bank, even call the president or head attorney and ask why this isn't closing. Clear up the title issue before signing any paperwork. You might consider including in your contract a clause that asks for liquidated damages (i.e., you receive compensation if this transaction can't close). Note that the inclusion of liquidated damages clauses is not valid in a lot of states, so talk with your attorney and ask how to avoid losing a deal due to an unclear title. It will depend on the answers to these questions: Was the contract contingent on being able to pass good title? Has the bank signed the contract?

If the deal falls through, you may decide to take steps to sue the bank,

Beware of Real Estate Fraud

Say you have a contract for $100,000. The investor who wants to buy this contract is willing to pay you $140,000, then fix up the property and sell it for $210,000. You're going to wholesale it and make $40,000, right?

You get ready to close on this deal within seven days. All of a sudden, you find out the seller can't pass on the title. But the buyer you've lined up has a contract with *you*, not the seller. The buyer is furious when she finds out. She calls and says, "I'm buying the house from you. Now you tell me it's not yours, that you're buying from this other guy. You didn't say that. You told me you were selling the house. I have a contract with *you*." You just attempted to sell something you didn't own; you may have committed fraud.

What should you do to prevent this from happening? Include a clear title clause in your contract. It would say, "This contract is contingent on being able to pass good title." I put this statement in big bold print, in plain English, at the top of every contract to protect myself against fraud.

with or without having a liquidated damages clause. For example, I would have made $30,000 on this transaction, so the damages would be at least $30,000, plus attorney fees.

Put All Disclosures in Writing

Disclosure means to make it clear to everyone involved in a transaction what you are doing. Certainly the one clear defense for fraud is disclosure. You have to be up front, careful, ethical, and honest in all your business transactions.

About the same year I started investing in real estate in Nashville, another guy a year older than I also started in real estate. I bought little houses and duplexes and I didn't understand wholesaling. I went out and borrowed money; I didn't use any of my own. I bought property and rented it out for more than the mortgage and did well. Great business, right? Tenants, cash flow, equity—awesome. I bought little houses and properties, as you might do in the beginning.

But this other guy had more guts than I did. He went around to some of the biggest commercial buildings in Nashville, and asked owners what they'd sell their buildings for. Most said they weren't for sale. But he persisted and asked, "Well if someone were to buy your building, what would you sell it for?" One small-building owner said, "We'd like $4 million for our building." The real estate investor replied, "Great. Will you sign a contract giving me a right to buy it for $4 million while I get all my partners and financing together?" This is typical in commercial property. His contract had a contingency clause so that if he couldn't buy it, he could withdraw from the contract.

Then he spent about $200 to run an ad in Germany stating commercial real estate buildings in Tennessee were available as a good investment. Some German investors who wanted to be property owners in the United States responded to the ad. They flew over to Nashville, he took them around to all the buildings on which he had contracts and asked, "What would you pay for this building?" They said they'd pay about $4.9 million, for example, on that particular building. He had a contract drawn up and signed. He put the deal together, went to closing, and repeated these steps. In two or three years, he made over $4 million by flipping or wholesaling about six buildings to German investors. He never owned the buildings, but he earned money by bringing the buyers and sellers together.

However, he got into trouble. He did something you're not going to do. The German investors thought that he was representing them, and they didn't realize he was making all this money, so they sued him and actually won a settlement, though not a full settlement for everything they'd requested. His mistake was in not disclosing everything he was doing in his contracts. He needed to explain in writing that he was putting the property under contract to resell it for a profit, so the sellers would know he's the middleman, not the buyer. His contract with the German buyers should have read: "I am a real estate investor. I don't represent you or your interests. I buy and sell property for a profit, and this contract is contingent on my being able to pass good title. I may or may not have good title right now." If that investor had done this with the German investors, he would have won in court because he would have disclosed exactly what he was doing. The German investors would have no doubt bought the buildings despite such a clause; they knew they would make a lot of money. The real estate investor who flipped, or wholesaled, the property still kept millions of dollars of property.

THINK ABOUT IT

What type of properties would you like to wholesale?

- Land
- Vacation property
- Apartment buildings
- Condos
- Homes
- Commercial property

If you spent 5 to 15 hours a week building a network of motivated sellers and potential buyers, how many properties could you wholesale in . . .

90 days? _____

Six months? _____

One year? _____

If you never make an offer on a piece of property, you will never own one. With proper disclosures and a contingency clause, your risk is minimized in making offers on good deals.

How many offers could you make this week? _____

This month? _____

Each month? _____

This year? _____

Have Lots of Deals Pending

At any given time, how many deals do most successful investors have in play? I probably have 14 to 18 deals in serious play right now and I know that half of them are going to fall through. I won't get the price I want; there will be a title problem or a money problem or some kind of

Five Minutes Late

Investing is highly competitive. There's a big investor in my town named Hal who helped me get started in real estate. Hal finds deals and sells them to me; sometimes I find deals and sell them to him. We exchange information. I call him and say, "Hal, what's this neighborhood all about? What are these properties worth? What about those apartments over there?" Like Hal, investors in your town can be of great help to you. They know the markets, and they are buyers and sellers. Get to know them.

One time, I went to a deal and arrived five minutes before Hal. In those five minutes, I got a signed contract. For about 30 seconds, Hall was upset for being late, and then he said, "Well, I've got to go. I'm looking at another deal today."

If you're in real estate, you have more deals and things to look at than you have time.

problem. I don't own them yet, but they're in play. Most investors have only one in play and they beat it to death. They follow it through and their fallout rate is 100 percent. Do sports teams go out and only play one game all year? No. Nor should real estate investors. Make lots of offers, do the numbers, and stick with it.

Research Property Values

One of my students, George, went out and found 42 town houses. He found out the seller wanted $46,000 for every town house, or $1.9 million for the 42 units.

Because the homes were in Maryland and neither George nor I knew real estate values there, I called an investor in my network who knows the neighborhood and asked, "What are 42 town houses in this part of Maryland worth?" He learned that they rented for about $700 a month and that investors pay $50,000 for those kind of town homes, though they are worth about $59,000 each. Knowing that, George offered $43,000 a unit, which would give him $3,000 profit each. He pockets a total of $126,000 for making some phone calls, finding a motivated seller, and putting the seller and buyer together.

Get That Signed Contract

Have you ever looked at a deal and said, "Gee, this is great! They're going to sell this house for $200,000 and I can sell it for $250,000. I'm going to make $50,000 and I know it's going to work. I've been over there 20 times. I've talked to them; it's going to be great." But after a week, you call the real estate agent and learn that somebody else put in a contract. You procrastinated and now it's gone.

Until you have a signed contract, you have nothing but dreams, so get that signed contract. As the old proverb says, "He who hesitates is lost."

Build Three Databases

Real estate is like almost any other business. Your income and wealth will be related to the activity you do and the people you know. Every business, especially real estate, is a people business.

To make deals happen without using your own money, you need just three simple databases, and you build them on a daily basis. Every time you talk to a Realtor, respond to an ad, or meet anyone in any situation, take time to find out which of the following three categories that person might fit into; as you make calls and talk to people, add their information to your databases:

1. Potential motivated sellers
2. Potential buyers
3. Sources of money

Here are some examples: "Oh you're a Realtor? Do you know of any good mortgage companies that lend money, or work with investors, or help first-time home buyers?" Perhaps you are calling on For Rent ads

Robert's Tip

I once responded to a newspaper ad (in the investment property section of a local newspaper) about an investment house for sale. It was worth about $90,000, and the owner sold it to me for $65,000 on owner's terms, with nothing down. I turned around and sold it to someone else for $10,000 down, with the buyer taking over the mortgage payments. I made about $100 a month for many, many years on this deal in addition to the $10,000 up-front profit.

When I went to the closing, I was feeling extremely happy. I had this great deal after being in the business only three years. For the first time, I asked the older gentleman, "By the way, do you have—or know of anyone who has—more properties for sale?" He said, "I'm so glad you asked. I've got 88 more." I wholesaled, or flipped, about 50 of his 88 properties and made a lot of money.

So remember this. If you're talking to an investor, landlord, or real estate agent, ask this question *every time:* "Do you have more properties?"

in the paper to find a motivated seller. You might ask, "You're an older landlord or landlady who's bought and sold a lot of properties. Do you want to lend money on real estate and make a 9, 10, or 11 percent return on your money?" If such people have funds to lend, you could borrow from them or they could become your money partners. Remember, you're always looking for potential deals, potential buyers, and potential sources of funding.

Within a few weeks of doing this, you'll have 10 or 20 names, addresses, phone numbers, fax numbers, and e-mail addresses in all three of those categories. Congratulations, you're now in business. Most investors calling on a For Sale ad are looking for a deal; if they don't sniff a deal, they hang up the phone. But you're looking for much more than deals—you want potential buyers and sources of funding, too. You're building a network of buyers, sellers, suppliers, and financiers.

Profit Margins

Profit margins on wholesale or flip deals will be different from each other, depending on the type of property, how well you negotiate, what deals you find, and the area you are in. Generally, on a single-family home, you ought to get the property for 20 to 30 percent below its market value. If a house is worth $100,000, you should get it under contract for $70,000 and make anywhere from $5,000 to $15,000 for wholesaling it. Then, when you flip it to someone else for $85,000 who fixes it up and sells it, he or she makes $15,000 on a $100,000 house.

I suggest making at least 10 percent of the gross, so if it's $400,000 you should make $40,000. Put it under contract for $280,000, sell it to

> ### Still Lots of Deals Around
>
> *You can never go broke making a profit.*
> **—ANONYMOUS**
>
> Sometimes I am interviewed on radio talk shows and callers tell me there are no deals left to be found. One caller had reviewed my book, *Unlimited Riches,* and decided I was out of my mind, saying, "Robert, you can't buy houses 20 to 30 percent below what they're worth." I explained that during the time that book was being written, I'd bought a $500,000 condo for $258,000. That was about 50 cents on the dollar. Maybe I should have said, "Yes, I am having trouble finding 20 and 30 percent below-market-value deals—because sometimes I'm getting 50 percent ones."

someone for $320,000. Of course, each deal is different and your results may vary.

Closing on a Flipped Property

There are several ways to close on a property that's been flipped, and four of them are described here: collapsed closing, one closing, assigning the contract, and putting the property under option.

Collapsed Closing

Here's how a *collapsed closing* works. You're buying a property for $200,000 and the lawyer deeds the property from the seller to you. At the same moment, there is a deed and a closing statement from you to the end buyer. The buyer comes in at 3:00 P.M. with mortgage money of $250,000. The funds are wired in or the buyer has a cashier's check and gives it to the attorney. The attorney takes the money and finishes the paperwork, then goes to the next room at 3:30 P.M. and gives the seller $200,000, pays off the liens, does the closing. A deed passes from the seller to you and from you to the buyer. The seller doesn't care what the deed says. He or she is interested in getting his $200,000. And you get $50,000 for being in the middle.

Wait a minute. We've got a problem. The seller paid all the closing costs of $2,000 for one transaction, and the buyer paid all the closing costs of $2,000 for the other transaction. Any excess closing funds should go to you, but you left out a statement to ensure that in your contracts. So the closing attorney has to follow contract law, stating there are two deeds and only one title insurance and there is double money here—another $2,000. What do you tell the lawyer to do with it? Read the contract. You just made $2,000.

One Closing

The other standard way is called *one closing*. There is one deed from the original seller to the end buyer; you are not in the deed. (That's preferable because mortgage companies don't endorse a property going from one person to another person in a day or a week.) The deed goes from the seller for $200,000 to the buyer for $250,000, and you get the difference. There is one closing statement, and you get a finder's fee.

Some mortgage companies don't like a middle person; they want the property to go from one person to the other without a flip fee. The process can be subject to fraud. Instead of getting a flip fee, call it a finder's fee, consulting fee, marketing fee, or some other fee that comes off the back of the closing statement similar to liens, taxes, attorney's fees, title fees, and survey fees listed in the closing statement. Now it says that a $50,000 fee, to you or your company name, is for finding the deal.

If that doesn't work, you can get the original seller to sign a debt and put a lien on the property for $50,000. The lien has to be paid off in order to pass title to the end buyer, so your finder's fee becomes a lien and comes off the back of the closing statement. Banks and mortgage companies generally don't care what comes off the back. But they don't want to see you buy a property for $150,000, which then goes to me for $200,000, and finally to a third party for $250,000, all within a short period of time. Instead, do a collapsed closing and take it as a fee or a lien off the back of the closing statement. Let your attorney help you out with that; that is how you get paid.

Assign the Contract

A better way to flip properties is to *assign your contract*. You have a contract to buy it from the seller for $200,000, and the buyer is willing to pay you $250,000, so have the buyer purchase your contract and you get $50,000. The wording says, "I assign this contract, the right to buy the house for $200,000, to you." Have you ever heard of the option market in stocks? There isn't any liability involved; the buyer simply bought your contract, just as people buy and sell the right to buy and sell the stocks. About a billion of them go around a day. You can do it with real estate.

Who Handles the Paperwork?

I always get a real estate attorney involved because if there's a mistake, that person is on the hook, not me. A lot of investors and seminars suggest you do your own paperwork, saying, "Here's a copy of this form; just fill it in; it's so easy." But I never do it because I don't do legal documents every day. What if I miss a sentence, or what if there's a new law passed a month ago? I want to work with an attorney who does this kind of paperwork every day.

Put the House under Option

One of my students never signs a contract to buy property; he thinks it's risky. He does between a half million and $1 million a year flipping properties by working the courthouse angle: He finds all the estate sales, probates, and foreclosures and puts them under contract and flips them. He has never owned a property, never hired a contractor, never borrowed any money. He's been doing this for six years. He simply flips, flips, flips.

His preference is to *put the properties under option*. The contract states, "I'll give you $10 for the right to buy the house for $200,000; I option it." That means he sells the option to the end buyer and lets the title company close it. If he doesn't end up buying that property, all he loses is $10.

You could make a fortune just doing options. For example, you option to buy a hotel for $10 million and then find someone who will pay $11 million and buy your option. You step out of it at the closing gong.

Pros and Cons

The good news about wholesaling is that it's fun; if you do it right, you really have little risk and you don't need any capital. You may need a little earnest money every now and then, but you don't really need serious money to start. Also, it's profitable.

Now here's the bad news. When you flip something, you make a nice profit, then you've got to flip something else; you've got to keep doing it, like sales. If you don't sell something next week, you don't get paid (unless you have set up some source of residual income).

Another disadvantage about wholesaling properties is taxes. If you buy and sell chairs and make a profit, you have to pay your normal income tax rate on whatever you make after all the expenses, plus you have to pay a self-employment tax, which is about 14 to 16 percent of what you make. When you work for a company, the company takes half of the taxes out of your paycheck and you pay the other half. So the government is going to get its 14 or 16 percent whether you work for somebody else or whether you work for yourself.

If you buy property (or anything else) with the intention of selling it for a profit, you're self-employed and charged a self-employment tax above and beyond your income tax. The way to reduce some of that is to write off everything you legally and ethically can so that on paper you can show less income and thus are taxed on less. If you decide to form a corporation that flips properties, then you can let the corporation write off things like business-related meals, travel, equipment, and driving expenses. Instead of paying out salaries, your corporation may pay out

THINK ABOUT IT

When you start your real estate business, you have your own enterprise that may allow you to write off a lot of expenses on your income tax form, both to start your business and to keep it going. When you work for someone else, your write-offs are very limited. As a business owner, you can use the government's money and less of your own to effectively make money.

If you're a new investor, use your newfound tax advantages. You may be able to deduct or write off all or some of the following as they relate to your business:

- Equipment
- Consulting
- Education
- Seminars
- Books
- Travel
- Phones
- Home office
- Interest on loans
- Depreciation of buildings you own
- Legal and accounting expenses
- Other business-related items

dividends, since dividends generally are taxed at a lower rate than salaries. Talk to your accountant. You could save a lot of money.

Don't forget to get a good accountant who understands real estate. You may even be able to write off the cost of this book!

Ask for Commissions

A few years ago, I had the chance to buy 14 duplexes. Another investor called me about them because he was overloaded at the time. He couldn't borrow the money to buy them because he had too much going on. I didn't even know what he had paid for them, though I later found out he actually had them under contract for $18,000 each. I could purchase them for $25,000 each. He would make $7,000 times 14, or $98,000, for flipping them to me.

I was going to buy them but I was overloaded, too. My credit was stretched out; some repair work was needed; I didn't want to deal with contractors. So I flipped these units. I found a gentleman who wanted to get into real estate and had some money. There were terms on this deal—specifically, they had a mortgage on them already that we could take over. All this buyer had to do was put down some cash and take over these loans; he didn't have to borrow a lot of money. I had them under contract for $25,000, and they were worth about $50,000. I flipped them to him for $34,000 each, making $126,000 ($9,000 times 14 units). It took a couple of weeks, some phone calls, some paperwork, and a bit of stress to make sure the closing went through, but at closing, I got a big check for $126,000.

Last year, these same duplexes were appraised at $120,000 each. Now this buyer is going to sell them and make more than $1 million. He's done well, and I'm happy for him, but I think that's not fair. If I hadn't found these deals, he wouldn't have made more than $1 million (in addition to what the monthly income and his tax write-offs). This deal has made him rich.

This upset me so much that I went home and started thinking. I said to myself, "When I go out and find a good deal, I ought to get paid for it." I declared I wouldn't do this anymore; I'm not giving away the ranch. Now, whenever I wholesale a property, I work the numbers backward. I say, "Mr. or Mrs. Real Estate Investor, when you buy these properties, what do you want to do with them?"

"Well, I'm going to buy them and hold them for 10 or 15 years and pay them off."

"Great. In 10 or 15 years, what do you think they'll be worth?"

"Property doubles; the debt will be lower. They'll be worth over $1 million."

"Great, so you'll make over $1 million."

Then I explain that one of the ways I get paid for finding deals is to take a percent of the selling price. I work backward, making the buyer feel good by showing how much money it's possible to make on this deal. For example, I'd say, "One of the ways I get paid is to receive a small percent of the profit when you sell or refinance the property. You wouldn't have had this deal if I didn't bring it to you. You wouldn't make this money if I didn't bring it to you." I have the buyer sign an agreement, almost like a second mortgage, that's recorded against the property. A lawyer draws up an agreement that says whenever this property is sold or refinanced, the seller (put in your name, your address, and phone number and keep the same address or a P.O. box) gets 5 percent of the sales price. Actually, I ask for 10 percent, because I'll take 5 percent and want to leave some room for negotiations. If you don't ask, I guarantee you'll get nothing.

Today, I'm getting a commission on 60 percent of the flips I'm doing. When those properties are sold or refinanced, the owners owe me money. The other day a lawyer called and said, "We're closing tomorrow on a property on 1013 Jones Street." I said, "I don't own 1013 Jones. Why are you calling me?" He said, "You've got this weird thing on the contract, recorded against the property behind the first mortgage, that says when it's sold, you get 5 percent. It's recorded; we can't close without you signing." I said, "Yeah, I flipped that house three

---

Robert's Tip

With these purchases, stay within reason and don't do anything that the market won't bear. If you're going to sell the house to them for $180,000, you could renegotiate the contract to $185,000 if you had to help them with the down payment.

Consult your own attorney and mortgage company to make sure you're not committing any violations or fraud. Some investors have obtained false appraisals for 30 percent higher than a house was worth and taken out loans on it—and that's fraud. Everything you do has to be legal and ethical. Check with your professionals to make sure it is.

Working with Appraisers

When you go to the mortgage company and you want to borrow as much money as possible, you certainly want the property to appraise for as high as possible. Work with the appraiser and declare that you really need it to be appraised high. "I think it's worth $350,000, but is there any way to ethically appraise it for more?" Perhaps you can help find some good comparable sales to support a higher appraisal. After all, real estate is not a science. It's an art.

Here's the other side of the coin. Go to the mortgage company to do a short sale. Say it has lent $300,000 on the house; you think it's worth $400,000. You tell the appraiser, "This piece of junk probably won't appraise for very much." Ask for a low number, around $200,000, so the bank will work with you. Don't commit fraud, and be reasonable, but there's usually a 5 to 10 percent fudge factor on most houses.

years ago." The lawyer sent me a check and a release to sign. If you plan to wholesale a lot of houses, try to get not only your up-front flip fee, but also a residual profit when the person you flipped it to sells or refinances it. Make sure it is a good deal for everyone involved.

Help the Buyer with Down Payments

If you're going to sell property, one of the major problems buyers have is coming up with the down payment. They need $5,000 or $10,000 down to buy your property. If you're selling them a property and making $30,000 or $40,000, you might consider helping them with the down payment. Either lend them a down payment or gift it to them. Some mortgage companies won't allow the down payment to be gifted or lent; they require it to be the buyer's money, in which case another option would be to buy something of theirs. They might have a motor-cycle, furniture, a TV, or collectibles worth thousands of dollars. This approach would be worth your while if you foresee making $30,000 by selling them a house, but they can't get a loan because they don't have a down payment. You would do a bill of sale that shows what you're buy-ing and for how much. Bring the bill of sale to the closing when the funds change hands. In the past five years, I've bought motorcycles, fur-niture, collectibles, cars, records, and watches, which enabled some of my potential buyers to get a down payment.

You can obtain down payments without using your own money to get a loan or property. If you don't want to purchase something or if you need a down payment, sell your services, sell something you have, or do a trade. Boats, cars, collectibles, something they want that you have. Almost every successful real estate investor I know has items such as cars, jewelry, TVs, and stereos they've acquired by wheeling and dealing in real estate.

CHAPTER 4

People are moved and motivated by emotions. Living is a constant process of
trying to satisfy emotional needs and wants.
—ROBERT CONKLIN

Lease Optioning

People dream of owning their own homes. Lease optioning can make it possible.

The Idea of Lease Optioning

If you rent a house or an apartment for $1,000 a month, what do you have at the end of the year? Well, $12,000 worth of canceled checks, right? Zip, zilch, zero. Everyone can use lease optioning. Even if you don't make a lot of money or don't choose to be a real estate investor, you can do one on your own house and stop throwing away your rent dollars. Would you like a vacation home? A house in the mountains or condo by the beach? You have a choice. You can pay $200,000, but what if after a year or two you don't like the place or you want to go somewhere else? You're stuck because you bought it. You might have to sell it, and what if the market has gone down? However, you could lease-option a vacation home. Stop throwing your rent dollars away, *and* stop using your own money to buy property.

Let's talk about cars for a minute. There used to be only two ways to buy a car. One way was cash: If you wanted the Camaro with the mag wheels and the flared fenders, and it cost $12,000, you could pay $12,000 in cash. Alternatively, you could borrow $12,000 from the car company or the bank if they'd lend you the money, but your payments would be high.

Today, about half of all cars are sold using a lease with an option to buy. You can get the new BMW for $42,000, or put $499 down and pay just $399 a month. People don't care about total price; they are more interested in the down payment and monthly outlay. We get excited when we see we can drive a Porsche for $2,000 down option money and $599 a month, because we tend to think of a $90,000 Porsche as unaffordable. Now, all of a sudden, it is.

Some wise businesspeople figured out they could lease-option cars. That means you drive it for two or three years and, if you like it and want to keep it, pay it off at a reduced price because some of your payments have already gone toward buying the car. It's a win-win situation. If you don't want to keep the car, you simply return it. Lease optioning offers the best of all worlds. Indeed, a whole industry has emerged out of this concept.

Well, I'm sorry to say that in your town, likely less than 0.02 of 1 percent of houses and condominiums are lease-option deals. Why? Because you haven't gone out there and done it yet. I've never seen more than 10 ads for lease-option houses in any big city, so you can create this in your own city. I also believe it's the answer to the problems associated with low-income housing, as it will definitely help poor people buy homes.

A Walk through a Lease-Option Deal

How do you find good lease-option deals? What's the best source? Look under Properties for Rent in the local newspaper. Every landlord or landlady who is renting properties has major complaints. They say, "Tenants bug me; repairs, repairs, repairs; it's a lot of work; there are lots of headaches." They rent properties for $1,000 a month but never *make* $1,000 a month because they've got to spend a lot of time and money fixing them up. They might be empty right now because the last tenants ran out on them. It's frustrating. Anyone in the landlord business has plenty of problems, headaches, and repair expenses.

If you could get them out of the repair business—and could ensure that they receive their checks on time every month so they can go on vacation—would they be interested in talking with you? Definitely.

Start by talking with them and finding their pain. Ask questions. How long have they had the property? How's the rental going? What do they rent it for? What have the repairs cost over the years? If you found the landlord through a For Rent ad, then the property is empty. If so, you'd ask these questions: How long has it been empty? One month? Two

Give Houses to Homeless Families

Consider a single mom who's been living in a shelter and can't qualify to rent anything. Her credit is wrecked; she's been homeless for a long while. Who wants to rent to someone with no current address and no income, whose credit scores are horrible, and who has had a job for only a short time?

Every year I go to a shelter and choose a single mom who has a job. She has no credit, no down payment, and can't rent anything. I find a house that's worth about $75,000. I buy it for $45,000 and put in a few thousand dollars worth of repairs. I borrow the $45,000; my payment on that loan is $350 a month. On the open market, the rent on that $75,000 house would be $700, but she couldn't afford that much rent even if someone over-looked her credit history.

Here's my strategy. I offer to rent it to her for $400 a month, which covers my loan payment. I also give her an option to buy it. She can buy it from me at my cost of $45,000. (I could also option it to her at $50,000 or $55,000 if I wanted to make a little money.) She pays the $400 a month, which I use to make the payment and escrow the remaining $50. At the end of the year, she's got $600 in savings. If people with bad credit pay all of their bills on time for one year, their credit rating goes to a B– or B+ score. That's not perfect (A or A+ would be perfect), but good it's enough to get an 80 to 90 percent loan to value in most cases.

There are programs in which the city and state banks want low-income people to buy homes and so will grant part of the money. Some programs create home ownership by training people how to become homeowners in free workshops, which I have the single mom attend. We have a written agreement that she has to keep a job, not incur any more debt, and pay her bills on time. We also show her how to start repairing her credit. In one year, she can buy the house that's worth $75,000 for $45,000 or $55,000. When she buys that house for $55,000, her payment will be about $400 a month for a 30-year loan at 6 to 8 percent interest. (She'll actually need a little more for taxes and insurance.) Now you see how you can make money and simultaneously offer good lease options to homeless people.

months? Three months? Last year, how often was it empty? What were the repairs? Have they enjoyed being a landlord or landlady or manager? Have they had any problems? What don't they like about it? What would they change about it?

Then work the numbers for the landlords you talk with and show them a solution in writing. For example, it they rent a property for $1,000 a month but it's been empty for two months, that means they're not collecting the full $1,000—they're really collecting about $700 prorated over the year. How much did they spend on maintenance and repairs? Say they spent $1,000 cleaning it and painting it. That means they're not making even $700 a month; they're making only $600 a month.

Work the numbers backward, both annually and monthly, for the past two or three years. Then ask them how much time they spend working on or worrying about the property. They might say about four hours a

THINK ABOUT IT

You might call some landlords and be told the units are always rented, they've always collected the money owed, and there have been no repairs. If that's the case, they are not likely telling the truth. But if that's what they say, then they don't have a problem you can fix. Move on. Follow the other For Rent ads in your newspaper and For Rent signs in your neighborhood for houses, duplexes, condominiums, commercial properties, shopping centers, and office buildings. You can lease-option any kind of property. Just pick what you like.

month—they had to drive over there and fix the commode. Is their time worth $10 an hour, $30 an hour, $50 an hour? Now the income isn't even $600 a month; it's $500 a month. Show them that, with all the work, all the headaches, all the problems, all the bills, they're really making only $500 a month as landlords.

Work the numbers. Say that landlord is making only $500 a month, and the market rent is about $1,000 (which you verified by calling some other property managers and landlords). Ask this question: "Mr. Landlord, if I could get you out of the repair business and get your money to you every time, what's the least amount you'd take per month?"

"Well, I rent it for $1,000, but it's clear I'm making a lot less than that."

Okay, you negotiate, negotiate, negotiate. Let Mr. Landlord speak first, but mentally know your ceiling price—the top price you're willing to offer. Maybe it's $650, maybe even $700, because you know you can rent it for at least $1,000.

Let's say your negotiations are weak and he insists on $700, that's it. You lease it from him for five years for $700 a month. That effectively locks in the rent amount for five years, too. Maybe you can lock it in for 10 years, even 20 years.

Now ask the least amount he'd take to sell this property, because you'd like to make an offer to buy it. Let's say you think the house is worth $100,000 and he responds to that question by saying, "I just had an appraisal. It's worth about $100,000." Because you're both investors, he might say, "I know you're going to make a lot of money, I'll sell it to you for $88,500." Well, that's not a good deal; it's is a bad deal because it's only 12 percent below what it's worth.

This *could* be a dangerous deal, but let me show you why it may not be such a bad deal. You could continue the negotiations by saying, "Mr. Landlord, if I pay you $700 a month, give me $150 a month credit toward the purchase price. That way, every month you make a payment, you get a bit of equity buildup or debt payoff, just as you would if you had bought it and borrowed the money." Also remind him how much the little repairs drove him crazy—the broken sinks and commodes and all that (which tend to be 70 or 80 percent of the repairs). You'll take responsibility for those repairs off his shoulders; the landlord will still be responsible for the big repairs, anything over $500 or maybe $1,000 or maybe $300—whatever you can negotiate.

In cases like this, landlords will ask for money down. Every property needs repairs, so let's say there are $3,000 worth of repairs. We'll get that taken care of, so instead of giving them $3,000 option money, you'll do the repairs. Who's really going to do the repairs? Your end buyer, not you; you are out of the repair business. You've gotten a landlord out of the small-repairs business. You have a five-year option to buy the property for $88,000, and it's worth $100,000. Horrible deal, $150 a month credit. Protect yourself: The question in your mind is, what if I can't rent this or sell it quickly? You're stuck. The property is currently empty, so negotiate delaying the first payment for 90 days or 100 days. What if they don't go for that? Try 60 days. What if they don't go for that? Try 30 days. Make a business decision.

Disclose everything you do in writing. Tell them you're a real estate investor—that you don't represent them or their interests, that this offer is based on your being able to remarket the property in the next 60 or 90 days. If you can't rent it in 60 days because the market is terrible and the house is horrible and you made a big mistake, you walk away. They're not any worse off, it's empty anyway—they're not making any money. Not everyone will agree to that disclaimer or contingency, but you'll get it most of the time if you ask properly.

Let's say you have 60 days. They signed a lease for five years at $700 a month, giving $150 a month credit, and you also have an option to buy it for $88,000 within the next five years, with some of the rent going to knock down that purchase price. How much money do you put down? Zero. How much money have you borrowed? Zero. How many contractors have you hired? Zero.

Clean up the yard and give the house a coat of paint to make it marketable. Then run an ad in the paper: "Easy qualifying, become a homeowner, stop throwing your rent dollars away, no banks involved, won't last." Create a sense of urgency. Have a voice mail people can call that describes all the attributes of the house. You think the house is worth $100,000. You think the market rent is $1,000 because you've done research—gotten comps and verified figures with property managers. Your phone might ring off the hook because now you can sell a house with easy qualifying.

The first responders call and say they'd like to buy this house; they're familiar with the neighborhood. The number one qualifying question to ask a potential lease-option candidate is this: "How much money do you have to put down?" Ask additional questions like these: "Do you have anything to sell? Any tax refunds coming? Any other sources of funds?" People often don't think about some of these things. Tell them you might get back to them and put their information in a file.

The second responders call and say they're looking to buy a house, but they don't think they can qualify. They don't have a big down payment, they have only $6,000. You can screen them over the phone.

Do a credit and criminal background check on everybody. Also screen them by sending them to your mortgage company and getting them prequalified. Explain how your home-ownership program works: They don't have to have perfect credit. They don't have to have a big down payment. But you need to check them out. Sometimes the mortgage company calls back and says your candidates are prequalified. Say the mortgage company has a 95 percent loan program for them, and they have enough of a down payment to proceed.

How much are you selling the house for? You thought it was worth $100,000. What's the actual difference if they pay $105,000 or $109,000 for 30 years at 7 percent? About $8 or $10 a month. So you write a contract for $107,000, in which they pay all the closing costs and fork over $6,000 as a down payment. They're happy. They didn't think they could buy a home, and you showed them how. Now you're ready to close.

Call the original seller. He wanted $88,000 but you can renegotiate that amount. As of now, $107,000 minus $88,000 means $19,000 profit in your pocket. And you already have $6,000 in option money. So you've received $6,000 plus $19,000 and you'll make another $13,000 at closing.

How would you like some extra money? Call up the original sellers and say, "Hey, I have five years." Always count it out, 2003, 2004, 2005, 2006, 2007. You'll give them $88,000 in five years; however, you're paying off some of the loan as you go, so it won't even be that much. Ask this question: "Would you like the money sooner?" They might say yes. If they receive the cash in the next 30 days, they tell you, they'd take a vacation, pay off bills, and so on. Great. Next ask them, "If you get that cold hard cash in your hands in the next 30 days, what's the least amount you'd take?" If they say $87,000, what do you say then? "Can you do any better?" If they won't, you agree to $87,000. You go to closing and sell it for $107,000. You just made $20,000 on a bad deal that you put no money into because you learned how to lease-option and do credit financing. You learned how to hustle, market, and take action.

Related Items

They put down $6,000 option money. Whose pocket does that go into? Yours. You don't pay taxes on it until it closes or the lease-buyers walk away from it. Hold onto it, because you may need that money to help close if they buy the house.

Second thing, your note to the original seller is $700 a month. You know the market rent is $1,000, but first ask these people the magic question: How much are they looking to spend per month? Well, they don't want to spend more than $1,100. You just got a $100 rent increase. They pay $1,100, and because you're a nice person, you give them $200 a month credit toward the purchase price every month, so they're not just throwing their rent dollars away. What's $1,100 minus $700 a month? $400 a month in your pocket if they continue to rent and not buy it.

- How long is their lease option? One-year lease, one-year option.
- They are responsible for the first $500 of repairs.
- Preapprove them. Do credit and criminal background checks. Get at least two landlord references from them.

Why two landlord references? If they're currently renting from Bill the landlord and they're bad tenants (e.g., drug dealers, don't pay the rent, tear the property up), what might Bill say? "Oh, they're great, man, I'm going to help move them over tomorrow. I'm loading their truck right now." But if they rented from Sue two years ago and didn't pay the rent, dealt drugs, tore up everything, Sue is likely to tell the truth because they no longer live in her property: "They don't pay the rent. They deal drugs. Don't rent to them."

Get the Option Money Up Front

What's the worst thing that can happen? Number one, six months go by, they don't pay the rent, trash the house, and they leave town. You have $6,000 in option money to do the repairs. It might take you $2,000 to $3,000 to paint the place and clean it up, so you make $3,000 profit, then lease-option it to somebody else, who puts $8,000 down and pays $1,200 a month.

Number two, most people don't lease-option their property because someone actually might buy it. A lot of landlords won't lease-option their rental property because, if someone actually buys it, they won't have it anymore. Get the money and go find another deal, right? I could sell all my property today and in three months I'd have better deals. So could you if you learn how to do this and get busy.

What's the third worst thing that could happen? A year goes by, they made the payments, and they leave. Great. Not a problem. You lease-option it again. Your debt goes down, you keep their option money, and they move on.

The Terms of Your Lease Option

If they miss a rent payment or are late by one day, they lose all their option money. If you rent out an apartment, what's the tenants' incentive to pay on time? Not much. If they're late, they pay a measly little late fee.

What's the number one complaint all landlords have against renters? They damage the place and don't take care of it. Are you shocked? Have you ever rented a car? You are no doubt nice, honest, and ethical. When you rent that car, how do you treat it? Do you drive over the bumps in the parking lot, take the curb, do some donuts? Let's floor it, see what this little rental car can really do, drink a Coke, throw it in the back seat, right? Don't we all tend do the same? Why? It's not that we're bad; it's just that it's not ours.

Perform Regular Inspections

How do you make sure that the property is not being destroyed and that your tenants are doing the repairs they are supposed to do? In every lease and lease option, you have the right to inspect the property every 30 days. I predetermine my inspection date in writing. For example, I say, "On the second Tuesday of every month, during business hours, I have the right to go in and inspect for repairs, check the air-conditioning filters, spray for bugs." Inspect it every 30 days; if you don't, you could be shocked at what you find.

When you lease-option, tell your tenants they're on a home-ownership program, that this is their house. They're going to fix it up. It's theirs. Way to go. They own it. They're buying it. They're lease-optioning it. They may plant some flowers, paint, maybe put a porch on the back. If they're homeowners, they take care of it.

- If they're late on the rent, they lose the option money.
- If they don't buy within a year, they lose the option money.
- If they do any damage or don't do the repairs, they lose the option money.
- If they don't close on a new mortgage within a year, they lose the option money.

In my landlord course, I explain that all my rent is due on the first of the month, late on the fifth, and we evict on the eleventh. This is my policy and procedure. I promise you if tenants can't pay this month's rent, they probably can't pay three months' rent if you let them stay in your rental property.

Do you remember when, during the Vietnam War, the Chinese captured some patriotic, red-blooded, dedicated Americans and put them on television and forced them to say "America is not a great country"? How did the Chinese torturers get them to do it? They used the psychological technique based on the idea that *if you put it in writing, you can't deny it.* They'd start out very generally and have them write a report detailing problems in America, and, of course, the valiant American POWs said there were no problems, no way, they wouldn't write, they wouldn't cooperate. Then the Chinese said, come on, there are race problems, poverty problems, *some* type of little problems. Just a little one, write it

THINK ABOUT IT

If your tenant-buyers don't pay the rent, how do you evict them?

This is where a lot of other seminars and books mess up. They recommend having a single lease-purchase contract. Never do that. Instead, insist on a lease contract and a separate option contract. That way, if they don't pay the rent, you can go to the eviction court with your lease. Judges understand leases. If judges see a lease-option contract, they might say, "Wait a minute, these people put money down, they're buying it. We can't evict them. You've got to foreclose on them." It's critical to create a separate lease agreement for that reason.

down on a piece of paper. Well, there are a few poor people in America. Then they get them to write some more: There are race problems, there are political problems. They'd write more and more, and after they wrote it, their captors would get them to read it. And after they read it, the Chinese would say, look, you just wrote that there are problems in America, and you cannot deny what you wrote in your own handwriting.

I believe if all contracts were handwritten, there wouldn't be lawsuits. "I didn't understand that I would lose the option money because it was in a big contract." Wait a minute, you have, in their own writing, "if I don't make my rent payment on time, I lose my option money." In all my lease options, I get the tenants to detail it in their own handwriting. If we go to court, the tenant-buyers cannot say that they didn't know about it, that they didn't understand, that it's too complicated. I get everyone to write in their own handwriting, "I understand that if I miss a payment, I will lose my option money. I understand if I don't do all the repairs, I will lose my option money. I understand that if I don't close on the house within a year with a new mortgage, I will lose my option money."

Say a month goes by and the tenant-buyer moves in, calls up, and says, "Oh my God, the commode is leaking, get over here and fix this thing." It happens all the time. We remind all our tenant-buyers about the lease option they signed. It says they're responsible for the first $500 in repairs and therefore they need to fix it themselves. They may say that's not fair, they don't remember that. We tell them we've got a copy of that agreement in the file; it's something they wrote in their own handwriting. They have a copy, too, but offer to read it to them, or ask if they want you to send them a copy. "Oh, ah, I kinda remember that." Having that paperwork will protect you. Make a point of getting them to write the agreement in their own handwriting.

If, after a year, they don't close on the house but they want to stay there, renegotiate the terms. Maybe get more option money or increase the rent. Real estate generally goes up, so if you control property for five years on a lease option, not only does the property value increase, but also the rent. How would you like to do lease options for 10 years? You lock in the price today for 10 years. Could you have made some money if you'd locked in 100 houses 10 years ago?

Lease-Option Plans

Are you ready to start lease-optioning properties? What kind of properties are you going to lease option? How many? Who are you going to call this week?

Call when you see For Rent ads. Ask those questions. Meet with land-lords. You can work with property managers, too, but it's a little different. Pay them their management fee because that's what they are interested in. Tell them you'll pay their fee and get them out of the repair business. How many properties would you like to lease-option in the next 60 days? How much money will you make each month? How are you going to get the properties to close? Get buyers preapproved with the mortgage company.

Here's an example of this. The last lease option I did was in Hermitage, Tennessee. One of my bird dogs called and said he saw a $200,000 house in a cul-de-sac for sale by owner. I called the lady and asked why she was selling. She said, "We really want to sell it. I know I could probably get a little more and sell it with a Realtor, but I am ready to move." I asked if the house needed any repairs. She said, "Yes it does. Would you like to come see it?" It smelled like a deal, so I drove 15 minutes to meet with her. She said, "I know this house is probably worth about $220,000; I don't want to use a Realtor and pay commission. My husband got transferred and moved away about three weeks ago; my daughter is apart from her dad, and I'm apart from my husband; it's a nightmare and we just want to go."

I asked her how much she needed. She said, "The mortgage on the house is $178,000. We need $3,000 to help pay for the moving bills and we'll move on." I told her I'd like to do a lease option; I disclosed everything in writing and told her that I'm an investor. Then I asked to see the repairs. She showed me the pantry door in the kitchen that had been scratched by a dog. She asked how she could trust me to make the payments, and I showed her my identity package. She actually called one of my references and then said, "Let's do it." My lease-option agreement gave me the right, in writing, to show the house and put a sign in the yard. I also disclosed to her that I'm a real estate investor—that I would be reselling it for a profit, and she understood that.

I got a three-year lease option and put $3,000 down, which I borrowed from somebody else. I called a few people and ran comps, and the house I thought was worth $220,000 was worth about $230,000. I ran an ad in the paper that said, "Stop throwing your rent dollars away. Become a homeowner, great neighborhood, easy qualifying."

I told the first caller how our program works. He drove by the house and was interested. I told him he had to contact our mortgage company and get preapproved. He went to the mortgage company, and my mortgage banker approved him right away. He bought the house from me for $237,000; it closed in 30 days; and we paid off the underlying loan.

The man who bought the house called me and said, "We had no idea we could buy a house. Thank you for getting us preapproved, Robert. This is great; we love the home and neighborhood. We thought we'd have to wait a year or two to buy one." They got into the home with very little down, and I gave them $3,000 toward the closing costs so they could qualify for a high loan to value. I don't mind helping them; I'm making a lot of money.

Ready for some advanced lease optioning? Shared equity. This is another way to buy property with no money down. Let's say you call on people who say, "We're not selling it. We're not leasing it. We don't want to lease-option it. Get out of here." Most investors will leave or hang up the phone. But you are going to ask another question: How about if I offer you a way to get your money and you have nothing to lose and no risk?" Say the house is worth $200,000 and they'll take $180,000 or $175,000 for it, but they won't let you option it, buy it, wholesale it, lease it, or get owner's terms. Ask them to give you an option to buy it for $180,000 and offer to split the equity. You'll become partners. If you sell it for more, you'll split the profit. If you don't sell it, nothing happens; they can still do whatever they're going to do.

So your backup plan on every deal is to get an option. If the people want $180,000, you'll give them $180,000 because you think you can get $210,000 after you do all the work, advertise, run around, and sell it. You're partners; you'll split the equity; you'll split the profit. You're better off; they're better off; it's a win-win situation. You can share equity with anybody. But you've got to go out there and hustle to make it happen.

Policies and Procedures on Lease Options

1. Write separate lease and option contracts.
2. Include repair contingencies and make sure the lease buyers understand they're responsible for minor repairs.
3. Make sure you are a named insured on the property. If the property burns, for example, you will get nothing if you're not the named insured.
4. Whose name is the house in? The original owners. That's okay, because you don't have any liability, but you may want to have them transfer it into a land trust or into your name.
5. Always ask for the deed; if you don't get the deed, lease-option it.
6. Record at the courthouse that you have an option on the property. Run your numbers and verify that your values and rents are correct, because you always want more money coming in than going out.
7. Do a title search to be certain that the person you are negotiating with is the decision maker and owner.
8. Confirm that the property taxes have been paid.
9. Run ads. Keep a constant stream of tenant-buyers. Screen, screen, screen them, and have them preapproved for financing.

CHAPTER 5

Things may come to those who wait,
but only the things left by those who hustle.
—ABRAHAM LINCOLN

Avenues Leading
to Motivated Sellers

If you do not find a motivated
seller, you can't begin to make money in real estate.

When people are selling a house and are eager to get rid of it, the only thing they care about is solving their problem. You may think they care most about the money involved. That's simply not true. You may think they want to sell a house. That's not true, either. This goes back to the most important question: Why do people buy a home? To spend a lot of money? No. Because it's good to buy a home? No. It's important to understand *why* people buy homes; then you'll understand why they *sell* them, and then you'll also know how to negotiate with potential motivated sellers.

Owning a home involves paying mortgages and spending money for taxes, insurance, and repairs. Many people could rent something for a lot less and live in a nice place with everything taken care of. But they buy homes based on the emotions of security and status, which is why some people live in houses that are too big and expensive for them. They also buy houses to get into better school districts for their children. But mostly, their decision has to do with emotion, not rationalization.

People also sell homes for emotional reasons. They either have a problem or they're avoiding problems. They have pain they want to "fix." They're getting divorced; they're getting remarried; they have to move out of the city or state; they're starting a new job. Sometimes, they have

Robert's Tip

One day, I called someone who wanted $480,000 for several houses. He said he had to have cash. The only thing on his mind was a $5,000 debt that had come due; he didn't have $5,000 to pay it, and the pain of the creditors calling him to pay his debt was becoming intense. He wanted to get rid of this debt. In addition, he didn't want the hassle, obligation, responsibility, and liability of managing the houses he'd inherited. He thought he wanted $480,000. He really only wanted $5,000. On the rest, $475,000, he took owner's terms. You have to find out what someone's real need or problem is.

It doesn't matter what your profession—people don't care whether you're a doctor, a lawyer, a real estate agent, an investor, an alien, or an illegal immigrant. They care about fixing their problems. As an investor, I'm rarely asked who I am or what my title or my job is. People don't care, and I usually don't tell them. Only offer the information they need and stay focused on solving their problem.

to sell their homes quickly. They may have to pay off the mortgage to have money to buy another home. Or they're in over their heads financially. Or they've had a change in their life—a divorce, a family debt, a job change, or money problems.

Your job as a real estate investor is to discover their problem and solve it.

Loss of job. Financial problems. Estate sale. Job transfer. Illness and no health insurance. Recent divorce or remarriage. Overextended credit, tax problems, tired landlords. These events can all lead to motivated sellers, because here's an example of what happens.

A homeowner has $400,000 in debt and the bank is demanding payment; the house may be worth $555,000, but the homeowner may not be able to get the money to pay off that debt or stop foreclosure. It's possible the home will be foreclosed and the owner's credit wrecked. You can help turn this into a win-win situation.

Perhaps all the sellers really want is to get $5,000 cash to pay off the bank and move. If not, they could be foreclosed upon and end up in real trouble. You could help the seller and the bank by putting the house under contract for $405,000—$5,000 to the seller and $400,000 to pay off the loan. Contact your network of buyers, investors, and real estate agents; perhaps you could find a buyer who would pay $455,000 for the $550,000 house. If it is a good deal, the buyers will come. At closing, the bank has its loan paid off, the sellers have been saved from foreclosure and have $5,000 to move, the end buyer gets a great deal, and you earn $55,000 (less any closing costs you had to pay) for finding a good deal and putting a buyer and seller together.

When people ask me whether real estate will always be a source of good deals, I say, "When people stop dying, stop getting divorced, stop falling into financial trouble, stop moving, and stop doing silly things, *then* there will be no more motivated sellers."

Signs of Motivation

You can look for signs of motivation by getting the Sunday newspaper and looking in the real estate section for places for sale. More specifically, look for the following sources of motivated sellers.

"For Sale by Owner" Ads

If people are trying to sell property and don't want to get a Realtor involved, it shows motivation to sell. Maybe they can't afford a Realtor, don't have time to get a Realtor, or simply want to sell it themselves. This can lead to getting a good deal quickly because you can negotiate directly with the decision maker.

Some investors just work with a list of properties; others work only with Realtors and make a fortune. Everyone is different. It all works. However, about 80 to 90 percent of the deals I do never go through a Realtor. They're never listed with the Multiple Listing Services. In the newspaper, you have nonlisted properties for sale by owner, and you also have listed properties that are for sale by real estate companies. You may be able to make a living by responding only to For Sale by Owner ads and asking them why they're selling.

"For Sale" Ads

These lead you to Realtors or to people who just listed their house for sale with Realtors. They'll likely try to get full price. These are probably not the best sources; sellers working through Realtors usually aren't motivated to sell at a discount, although you might find some motivated sellers in this group if you are willing to make enough calls.

Expired Listings

Expired listings can be a good source of deals. Contact some real estate agents and ask them to help you make offers on all of the listings that have expired or are about to. For example, let's say someone listed a house for sale with a Realtor for $300,000. The Realtor listed it for six months and it has not yet sold, but the agreement expires at the end of six months. Chances are the seller might now be more motivated. Do you see how this list could be a source of some good deals for you?

Investment Properties Ads

Who would list properties for sale under the category of investment properties? The following describes several possibilities.

Investors and Their Brokers

Investors can be understanding toward other investors, so sometimes they sell the property for below what it's worth. Or maybe the property was purchased 30 years ago and hasn't been fixed up or managed properly. You might be able to buy it for less than market value because the seller is motivated.

Landlords and Landladies

Those who have been in business for a long time, especially, may be motivated sellers. Being a landlord can be tough, tiring, and stressful. Often, small-property owners don't have systems and management policies and procedures in place. They may have been lax about collecting all the rent; maybe they haven't been raising the rent; perhaps they haven't been keeping up with the maintenance and the property is in disrepair. They likely bought it 20 or 30 years ago for very little money, and they may not understand today's real estate market as well as they should, so they'll sell it for below market.

"For Rent" Ads

When you call on For Rent ads, you get in touch with landlords or landladies, real estate investors, property managers, or Realtors acting as property managers. Landlords and landladies are excellent sources for investment property and lease-option deals. (See Chapter 4.) Everyone who owns rental property knows that all of the tenants pay the rent on time and never call about repairs, right? Wrong.

Robert's Tip

Remember, everyone you talk to has three things to offer you: (1) They might have a property for sale. (2) They might be a buyer and become part of your network of investors, buyers, and Realtors who buy some of your good deals. To build your list, every time you call on a deal, ask, "Do you ever buy any properties, or do you know anyone who buys any properties?" And (3) they might be a source of funds. They may lend you money to buy real estate.

Landlords have rent collection problems, repair problems, vacancy problems; they can be constantly dealing with headaches, but they can be highly motivated to sell. If you talk to 20 to 30 small-property owners, managers, landlords, and landladies, you'll probably find some deals, and they often have more than one property to sell.

Auctions

Auction companies announce that they're auctioning a house, a commercial property, or a farm 30 days from now. You want to call that auction company, gather all the details, and get on its list to be invited to the auction. You also want to meet dealers at the auction company because they're out to find deals like you are. They find motivated sellers who are willing to auction their property. Sometimes those sellers say, "I don't want to auction; I don't want to advertise; I don't want to pay your auction commissions. But do you know of anyone who will buy property quickly?" Many auctioneers are also brokers and sell a lot of property, so try to develop good relationships with them.

Other Investors

You can meet other investors at auctions because, when you buy at an auction, you usually have to close within 10 or 20 or 30 days with cash. Would you like to know a lot of investors who are looking to buy properties with cash? Absolutely, because when you find a deal, you can wholesale it to them; you can partner with them; you can use their funds, their cash, their credit. They're your real estate partners. Again, as in any business, networking is invaluable. Go to every auction, meet everyone, and add them to your database.

Legal Notices

Newspapers post legal notices of divorces, bankruptcies, and foreclosures. Follow all of those and get to know who the players are. Call them; look at the deals. Find attorneys who are representing people in bankruptcies, divorces, and foreclosures and see if you can contract any of their deals. Call a few lawyers and ask where they advertise foreclosures and bankruptcies. Get a copy of that paper and go to work.

Obituaries

This may sound a little morbid, and I prefer not to do it, but some of you might. In the newspaper, look for a list of people who have just passed away. These people may have owned property, but their family members often live in other communities. You can perform a service for that family by helping them liquidate the real estate. They don't want it;

Executors Appreciate the Calls

When my grandfather, may he rest in peace, passed away, he owned a condo in Miami. Like many families, we lived in another state. No one in my family, including cousins and grandchildren, wanted to visit the condo: We didn't want to see it without my grandparents there.

My father, the executor of my grandfather's will, was thankful that a real estate investor in Miami read the obituaries and offered his services. My father not only offered him the condominium, but also the car and the furniture. My father knew exactly what the condo was worth, but he sold at a deep discount. I'm sure that the investor who sold it made a lot of money. Even though we're in real estate ourselves, we were thankful that this investor offered us the service of dealing with this property.

they usually don't know how to sell it; they certainly don't want to take a lot of time to make decisions. You could offer them a quick sale and they might be motivated.

If you contact them, of course, be sensitive to what they are going through, saying, "I'm sorry to hear about Rose passing away. Is this a good time to talk?" Ask them whether property is involved and what they plan to do about it. Could you help them by offering to get rid of it quickly? If you call on enough obituaries, you'll probably get deals.

Small Newspapers

You can also run classified ads to find deals. You can run them in newspapers, on radio, TV, and billboards. Do you have any local neighborhood shopping newspapers, community weeklies, or even the *Thrifty Nickel?* Putting ads in these small papers doesn't cost much—$10, $20,

---

"I Don't Want It"

William, one of my students, took it a few steps further after he read in the paper that one of the wealthiest businessmen in town had died. The deceased had started some restaurant chains and had accumulated a lot of money—a very good man. A few days later he called the wife of the deceased and said, "I heard you had some real estate. Would you like to sell it?" The widow said, "My husband had all this property, all these apartment buildings, all these duplexes, and it drove him nuts. I don't want it, just come and get it." From that phone call, my friend got 14 deals under contract for about 50 cents on the dollar—just because he read that obituary and took action.

Robert's Tip

If you read the local paper every day, you'll learn a lot about pricing, about Realtors, about the market, and about rents, so read it faithfully.

Every time I go to a new town, the first thing I do is open the real estate section and start circling ads, just to see what deals are there and what prices are like. If you do this enough and make enough calls, you'll find deals, guaranteed. In fact, the best deals I've found over the years came right out of the real estate section. One was a commercial property I wholesaled and made a lot of money on. I found it in the *Miami Herald*.

When I called the broker who ran the ad, I asked, "How many people have called on this ad?" Now, Miami has three giant real estate associations with hundreds of active real estate investors—thousands of Realtors everywhere. It's a highly competitive, hot market. But the broker told me he'd received only three phone calls. What was everyone else doing? What should you be doing?

$30, or $40. One of my students did a study in Memphis, Tennessee, and found that—per time and per dollar—people get a much better response out of the smaller neighborhood newspapers than they do in the larger papers.

Use the following sample "I buy houses" ads:

DO YOU NEED A MONEY MIRACLE RIGHT NOW? If you have a house in any condition that you want to sell, I've got cash, know-how, and banking connections. And I'm eager to buy your home. Please call [investor's name] at 000-0000 right now for an extraordinary no-risk proposition.

ARE YOU STARVED FOR CASH? Do you have a house you want to sell? I've got cash, know-how, and banking connections, and I'm itching to buy your home. I urge you to call [investor's name] at 000-0000 right now for an extraordinary no-risk proposition.

ARE YOU BEHIND IN YOUR HOUSE PAYEMENTS? Do you want to sell your house? I've got cash, know-how, and banking connections, and I'm itching to buy your home. I urge you to call [investor's name] at 000-0000 right now for an extraordinary no-risk proposition.

Legal Newspapers

Every major city has a legal newspaper in which people advertise bankruptcies, foreclosures, divorces, estate sales, probates, and related events. Get a copy of this newspaper and look at it at least once a month. Then follow up with phone calls.

Weekend Research Outing

It's always better to drive for dollars with one other person. For example, every Saturday or Sunday, my friend Hal and his wife get in the car and go on a scouting outing. For them, it's like a date. She gets a pad of paper and a pen while he drives slowly. They look for signs of motivated sellers (as described in this chapter) and she writes down addresses. In two or three hours, they glean 50 to 150 addresses. Then they do their research. They call the registrar of deeds, do a computer search, try to find the owners, and send letters to those owners. It's work, but it's worth it because Hal makes between $8,000 and $15,000 on an average flip.

> ### Robert's Tip
>
> In the next 14 days, take two to four hours on a Saturday (or any afternoon that works for you) and drive for dollars. Write down addresses and follow up with the registrar of deeds, contact a Realtor, and/or access city and state tax records. Find the owners; call them up and write a letter. Please note, I didn't just say call them up. I didn't just say write a letter. I said call them *and* write a letter, because your response rate will be higher. When you call, say, "I saw your property. Would you like to sell it? What would you like to do with it? What are your plans? How long have you had it? Go with your basic analysis and, when you write a letter, say, "I might want to give you cash for your house. Please call." If you write a letter *and* make a phone call afterward, you'll have a much better response. Test it for yourself!

Foreclosure Attorneys

In every area, you'll find two or three attorneys who specialize in fore-closures. Find out who they are and talk to them They may not be able to give you a lot of information because of client confidentiality, but they might be interested to know someone can buy their properties, pay off the banks, or help their clients get rid of their properties.

Driving for Dollars

Pick an area that's in transition: one that is getting better or an area where people are fixing up houses. Watch for lots of activity—houses for sale, houses for rent. Then start driving around looking for signs of possible motivated sellers: vacant homes, needy homes, condemned homes, For Sale signs, For Rent signs, For Sale by Owner signs. You ought to get excited if you see gutters hanging off, 10-foot-high grass, garbage

Robert's Tip

I want to save someone's life here—not only in real estate, but in general. Are you ever scared about getting attacked or robbed or car-jacked or worse? It often happens because people aren't aware of who's around them when they get out of their car or are walking around. Someone pulls into a parking lot or garage or up to a vacant home. If you had looked, you might have seen that bad person hanging around, or you'd see two or three suspicious-looking people on the corner. If you're driving around neighborhoods or pulling up to vacant homes, *always be aware of your surroundings,* and don't get out of your car unless you feel comfortable.

piled up, holes, junk cars. There's a basic premise to follow: The worse shape the house is in, the better the deal. These are the signs of opportunity. Write down the address, locate the owner through the property tax records, and phone or write them to see if they want to sell.

One of my students in his early twenties, a young man in Memphis, Tennessee, just sends letters to homeowners of vacant properties he finds driving around—about 50 to 100 letters a week. He had been making $25,000 a year working part-time on the night shift, but he made that much *on one real estate deal.* He has now made about $200,000 in 12 months just using this idea consistently. He doesn't work the night shift anymore.

Signs

Here's another law of the real estate universe: The smaller the For Sale sign in the yard, the better the deal. There's probably no competition since no one can read the phone numbers on the sign!

Sign behind a Bush

I was once driving down the road and thought I saw a For Sale sign in the window behind a bush. I got out of the car, climbed through the bush, and could read only five of the seven numbers. I actually wrote down every possible number the sixth and seventh one might be. I made about 40 phone calls before reaching the seller 30 minutes later. (Most people would be deterred by having to do all that phone work.)

I finally hit the right number and said, "Hey, do you have that house for sale over on Joseph Street? Has anyone else called on it?" He said, "Nope, you're the first one in five months." That's because nobody could see the sign! But I did see it. Before long, I was able to buy the property for about 40 cents on the dollar.

Before we ended our conversation, I asked the magic question, "Do you have any others?" He said, "Yes, one on Fatherland Street." When I drove over there, I found his sign buried about a foot and a half in the dirt. It'd fallen off the window. Can you guess how many people had called on that ad? None. That house was worth about $100,000 and needed about $10,000 in work. I got it under contract for $55,000, wholesaled it, and made about $20,000.

Foreclosures

Say a house is worth $500,000 and 20 years ago the bank lent $400,000 on it. Today, the mortgage is down to $250,000. The property has been foreclosed on and the bank has to take it back. The bank now reluctantly owns the house but would prefer to have its money back. Bank officers in charge of these properties are highly motivated to sell that house. They're under strict federal and state guidelines to maintain a specified amount of money in reserve. If they have too many

---

Robert's Tip

If you ever want to sell a house, use some basic advertising intelligence and get a big sign with big numbers so people can actually see it. I have an eight-foot sign that wouldn't fit in a car, and I use flyers and balloons and flags so anyone driving within three blocks can see it. Of course, there is a disadvantage—kids love to throw rocks at my signs because they're such big, easy targets. How big will your For Sale sign be when you are ready to sell something?

---

foreclosures and repossessions, it messes up their banking and lending ratios. Often they'll sell one of these properties for a discounted amount. Since they're passing deals along to somebody, that somebody should be you.

Foreclosures are a matter of public record. They're listed in the newspapers because the people involved are required to publicize them.

You can call up a real estate attorney and/or title company in your area and find out where foreclosures are listed. Start getting to know the people involved, including buyers with cash who attend sales. Be sure to go to some foreclosure sales and meet everyone there. Get to know them, find out what they're looking for, and put them into your database, possibly under all three categories: They find deals; they buy deals; they have funds because they're cash buyers. Eventually, you and your money partners could buy at the foreclosure sales, because there are deals there. If someone else buys a deal at the foreclosure, talk to that person. Maybe he or she wants to resell the property, or perhaps you could be partners.

Short Sales

Let's say that a bank or mortgage company has written a loan for $100,000 on a house that now qualifies for foreclosure. The loan is $100,000, but the financial institution does not want to take back the property. Sometimes, especially with the high foreclosure rates occurring in many parts of the country, the institutions will discount, or *short*, the amount of the loan to get rid of it. If the house is in the process of foreclosure or has been foreclosed on, the bank may be willing to take only $70,000 to $90,000 on the $100,000 loan. Often, you must present an appraisal on the house as well as a repair list so that the institution can justify taking less money. Be persistent, especially in finding the right department and decision maker at the bank.

Right now the foreclosures in some areas of the country are up 100 to 200 percent. When the economy slows down, people who overborrowed and overspent during the good times have a financial hangover that leads to foreclosures. And the banks that have lent too much money have to take back property. It's an ongoing cycle.

No matter where the economy is in the cycle, there's opportunity to make money. In the current climate, banks have foreclosed on so many properties that if they are owed, say, $250,000 on a foreclosed property, they're tremendously eager to move that property off their books, and they'll short-sell the mortgage. That means you could offer less than the mortgage amount and buy the property as a short sale.

First, you need to determine which bank owns the foreclosed property and negotiate with the head of the real estate loan department or someone who can make a decision. (The clerks who answer the phone probably can't help you; it can take a while to find the right person.) You can find out what the property is worth from the loan amount, how long the bank has owned it, and so on. Then ask if the bank will sell the house at a discount.

Many investors have been able to buy properties from 20 to 60 percent below what they're worth by doing short sales with the banks. Many are wholesaling these great deals to other investors, or they may have partners with good money or credit who help them buy and hold these great deals. This is another way to make money in real estate without using your own capital or credit.

Tax Sales

Say you own a house that you purchased for $200,000 some years ago, putting $20,000 down and borrowing $180,000. You have a first mortgage of about $175,000, and the house is now worth $500,000.

This level of appreciation has taken place in many markets. Say you go to your bank and get a second mortgage for $100,000. Now you have a first mortgage of $180,000 and a second mortgage of $100,000. Your bank calls and says, "We suggest you get one of these secured credit card equity lines and pay off your car loan and your Visa bill, which will make your debt tax deductible, because Visa payments and your car lease or car payments are generally not tax deductible." You follow the bank's suggestion and take out an equity line on your house, secured by real estate, which now becomes deductible, and pay off your other debts. You now have a third mortgage on the house for $40,000.

Then you decide to go into real estate and want to borrow $50,000 from your mom to get started. She says, "I want a written loan contract and security." You go ahead and acquire a fourth mortgage for $50,000.

Unfortunately, you get divorced. The court decrees that you owe money to your ex, which you can't pay, so your ex gets a judgment against you for $30,000 and files it against your house. You owe $8,000 in property taxes, but you forgot to pay them last year and you can't pay them this year, so the city puts a $16,000 tax lien against your house. If you don't pay these taxes, the city will foreclose on it.

Now things are really getting bad and you can't pay any of the debts. Who is first in line for the debts owed? The city. Property taxes are always paid first. Now the mortgage company could show up and pay the $16,000 in taxes to protect their $180,000 or $100,000 mortgage. But banks and finance companies sometimes don't do the smartest things. Often the properties go to tax sales and are foreclosed on. Call your local tax collector's office and get a list of properties with tax liens. Then call the owners; they may be motivated. Also, go to tax sales and start learning about them. The tax office may have property that no one bought at the sale. See if you can get a good deal. Contact a local title lawyer to learn the ins and outs of your local tax sale rules.

Home-Saver Program

You can help homeowners save their homes if they get behind in payments and face foreclosure. You can help the homeowner/seller catch up on payments, buy it using owners' terms, set up a lease option, or flip it. Using a home-saver program, you work with mortgage companies, credit counseling companies, housing authorities, and nonprofits. Here is how to talk to potential sellers.

It's important to ask these questions before deciding to take action:

"Why are you selling?"
"How long have you been trying to sell the property?"
"Is the property in your name?" (Make sure you negotiate with the decision maker.)
"What is the mortgage amount on the property?"
"What's the least amount you would take for it?"

After a price is stated, ask how they came up with that number. You'd be amazed how people come up with their values.

In this process, pretend you're Colombo. Whenever they say anything, ask another question. Why? How? If they're reluctant, remind them that the purchase price, when they bought it, and the amount of the mortgage is public information. By now, you're taking on the role of a real estate doctor. In order to help someone, you need information, so keep asking more questions.

"How old is the house?"
"Are mortgage payments current or in arrears?"
"If in arrears, by how much?"
"What are the taxes?"
"How much is the insurance?"
"By what date do you have to sell it?"
"How much would the house rent for?"

"Does the house need any repairs? How are the roof, ceilings, windows, walls, floor, plumbing, stairs, carpet, kitchen, bathroom, basement, yard?"

"How much would repairs cost?"

And the million-dollar question: "Do you have any others?"

Always ask the sellers if they know about any other properties. You could even run a classified or display ad like this:

> **Home-Saver Program—Save your house
> from foreclosure. Call now, 000-0000.**

CHAPTER 6

*Money is always there but the pockets change; it is not in the same pockets
after a change, and that is all there is to say about money.*
—GERTRUDE STEIN

Ways to Source Funds

Most people who invest in real estate make money in only one or two ways: They buy properties and borrow money from the bank to do so, or they deal in mortgages. But many more sources for funding and profiting from your real estate investments exist. You can use these sources of funds to buy property. Do not use your own money. Create money from other sources to get into real estate.

Mortgage Origination

If you're actively buying or selling property, you're initiating, referring, or acquiring mortgages. It's customary to be paid for these services by affiliating with a mortgage company, a mortgage broker, or network marketing companies that do mortgages.

Affiliate with some good mortgage brokers or become one yourself. Go to a variety of mortgage companies—at least one main company plus two or three secondary ones—and research the best deals available at a given point in time.

Investors (and others) who attract customers needing a mortgage are called *mortgage originators*. Originators are paid anywhere from 30 to 70 percent of the up-front fees on a mortgage—just for marketing and bringing in customers. For example, if a mortgage broker is working on a $200,000 mortgage that has two points ($4,000), the originator would receive half, or one point ($2,000), for filling out the application and helping to start the loan process. I suggest you should get about half, or at least 20 to 25 percent, of the points for referring mortgages to a mortgage company. A lot of times, you can actually become an employee of the mortgage company, so you don't have to be licensed. (Since every state is different, check with a local mortgage company about these requirements. Also note that in some states, paying fees to mortgage originators is illegal.) Please send me an e-mail if you want to learn about affiliating with a mortgage company, My email is: robertshemin@the-beach.net.

Referral Fees

You can also negotiate for marketing, referral, or consulting fees as you develop marketing relationships with mortgage companies and brokers.

Make arrangements to receive something in exchange for bringing in customers—either money or goods (a desk, computers, etc.). Make this a worthwhile way to legally and ethically bring in rewards for your valuable referrals.

For the first five years I was in real estate, I often referred people to service providers I knew and trusted. In fact, I'd refer 40 to 60 mortgages a year to the best mortgage company I could find. When I decided I wanted remuneration for these referrals, I went to the decision makers at this mortgage company, who agreed to pay me 50 percent of the referral fees. The company keeps the other 50 percent for its efforts. This is a fairly standard commission. The originator, the person who brought in the business, gets about half of the profit or points.

You can apply this concept to related services, too. For example, you can develop referral relationships with insurance agents for your contacts who need renters' or homeowners' insurance. You can also refer them to contractors or people who do repairs in exchange for a fee of 10 to 20 percent. By doing so, you provide a service that brings business to them that they wouldn't otherwise have had. You deserve compensation for that service.

However, be sure to handle your referral fees correctly. First, put every detail of your agreement in writing so it's clearly understood by everyone involved. Specifically spell out the amount of your fee and exactly when and how it will be paid. Second, make sure you have no liability in the arrangement you set up. For example, if you refer a certain contractor, make it clear that you don't *guarantee* his or her work. In fact, encourage your contacts to do their own research beyond your referral.

Referrals on title work can be another source of fees. Some large real estate companies get referral fees from title companies for sending them customers—approximately 20 percent of the title closing fees. For this example, assume the title insurance premium on a $500,000 house was between $1,500 and $3,000, with 70 to 90 percent of that being profit to the title company. It charges closing fees of $200 to $500 and document preparation fees of $50 to $200. Therefore your referral fee could be 20 percent of the title, premium, and some or all the closing costs.

I suggest you find a good title company and negotiate referral fees with the decision makers. After all, other real estate investors are doing this and making good money doing so.

THINK ABOUT IT

Whether you are a beginner or a pro, how many deals might you be involved in doing during the next . . .

One year? _____

Five years? _____

Ten years? _____

Twenty years? _____

If you could get referral fees for mortgages, closing and title services, repair and contractor services, property insurance, consulting, and/or any other services your buyers and sellers might need, how much could you make? _____

Let's say you are involved in 20 properties and/or sales in the next year. If you got a mortgage referral fee of only $500 per loan, that would be an extra $10,000 to you. Do the math.

Banking Relationships

A great source for buying property is through banks. If you have some good deals, a good business plan, and some good credit, getting funds from a bank may enable you to buy property without putting any of your own money into the deal.

Here's how I bought over 100 properties without using my own money: I went to a bank and got a $100,000 line of credit secured by my own house. The bank also agreed to do 15-year loans on any property I owned at a 75 percent loan to value. That is, if a house had a value of $100,000, the bank would lend $75,000 (75 percent).

For example, I would find a deal that was worth $100,000 from a motivated seller who would sign an offer to sell it to me for $70,000. I would use the bank's money (the line of credit) to pay the seller cash of $70,000. One month later, when the house looked better and I had rented or lease-optioned it, I would ask the bank for a permanent 15-year loan. The house would appraise for at least $100,000. The bank would lend me $75,000 (75 percent), which I used to pay off the loan, or put back into my line of credit. Then my line of credit was back at $100,000 to pay cash for another house. Not one cent of my own money was used. Caution: *Never borrow money you are not positive that you can pay back.* Also, be careful about borrowing against your own home; if the loan is not paid back on time, you could lose your home.

If you do not have great credit or the ability to do this, find someone who does have that ability. Whatever you lack in business, find someone who can help you. You probably know or can find people who want to make money in real estate and have great credit, but who don't have the time, energy, or knowledge to make it happen. You can develop the knowledge and use your energy to find the deals. Let others borrow the money. You can partner with them 50-50, 60-40, 70-30, or whatever works for both of you.

Always make sure you have a good deal lined up before you borrow any money. Have a built-in cushion, too, as well as an exit strategy. If someone else is borrowing the money for your deals, make *triple* sure it's a good deal.

Also begin establishing good relationships with a bank. When I started out, I went to the bank almost every month to ask for a loan. Every month the answer was no. Then, the fifteenth time, the answer was maybe, and soon after it was yes. The bank gave me a $50,000 loan on a duplex worth $80,000.

At that time, I had more money on deposit in the bank than I was able to borrow. But the way banks work, after you borrow once, you can borrow again—and then again. You may find that when you borrow only $100,000, the bank doesn't really care about you. But when you borrow

---

Robert's Tip

I challenge you, regardless of the status of your money or credit, to fill out a financial application, go to a bank or mortgage company, and get pre-approved to buy something. It's a good exercise to see where you stand. I'm not saying go out and borrow money; I'm saying start building that relationship. Then you'll find out what you need to do to improve your credit and be able to borrow funds.

---

over $1 million, the bank cares! Loan officers start calling—how are you feeling, how's business, let's go to dinner, and so on.

Hard Moneylenders

You'll find hard moneylenders in every major town. These people have a lot of money (or access to it), and they may lend it to you—at high interest rates—on the deals you want to buy. They don't care much about your credit. For instance, if the mortgage rate today is 6 to 8 percent, some hard moneylenders may charge 10 to 15 percent. And instead of charging one or two points (i.e., 1 or 2 percent of the loan amount) like a bank or mortgage company would, they charge between 2 and 10 points. If you want to borrow $100,000, a hard moneylender might charge a $10,000 fee plus 15 percent interest to borrow money for that home. Obviously, if you already have the cash or have good enough credit to satisfy the bank, borrow the money you need elsewhere. Going to a moneylender is a last resort.

The biggest advantage of getting funding through hard moneylenders is that they really don't care about your credit. Plus they can respond quickly, while banks and mortgage companies are still collecting four wheelbarrows full of paper and taking 30 or 90 days to process your loan.

You always want a source of hard money in case a bank won't fund your promising and profitable deals. So your homework is to look in the newspaper for ads that say "We Lend Money," then meet with two or three of these lenders and develop good relationships in case you want to borrow from them in the future. Also, go to your local real estate

> **Robert's Tip**
>
> Don't be greedy. If you stand to make $30,000 on a deal and can get it done quickly and easily by paying a hard moneylender $5,000 in points and interest, so be it. A lot of investors say, "I'm not going to pay that much interest. That's too much." But, moving forward, the important question to ask is "How much will I make on this deal?"
>
> Never let cost get in the way of profit. If it's profitable, do it.

investors association meeting to meet other investors and lenders. (And check out www.robertshemin.com.)

Property Owners

I suggest you learn every possible way to finance mortgages and use them so you are never stuck *not* being able to do a deal because you don't have access to funds.

Normally, when you buy a house, you get a new mortgage to buy it. If the house costs $1 million, you borrow $900,000 and put $100,000 down. Depending on your credit, income, and the collateral or property, the bank or mortgage company will determine how much it will lend you. A homeowner's loan, meaning you are going to live in the property, is less risky for a lender than a loan for a non-owner-occupied property or an investor loan. People are less likely to default on a home loan and risk losing their residence. Of course, there are hundreds or thousands of loan programs out there. Here are a few that may be of interest to you:

- There are many 100 percent homeowner loans for people with good credit.

- For first-time home buyers, there are special city, state, and national programs that don't require borrowers to have much of a down payment, even if their credit is less than perfect: They may need only $500, $1,000, $3,000, sometimes $0 down.

- Home buyers with marginal credit who are going to live in a house can sometimes get a 70 to 80 percent loan to value. That is, if they find a house worth $100,000 for $80,000, they might be able to get a loan for the entire $80,000, or 80 percent loan to value. Some lenders might require them to put in some of their own cash as a down payment.

- Home buyers with bad credit can often get loans that are 65 to 75 percent loan to value.

- Real estate investors or nonowner occupants can often get loans on single-family homes, duplexes, or buildings with up to four units at 90 to 100 percent of their value. They must have excellent credit and good verifiable income.

- Many investors who are self-employed can get 70 to 80 percent loan to value if their credit is good.

If you negotiate a good deal on a property, you might be able to borrow the entire amount. If the house is worth $100,000 and you can buy it for $75,000, you may be able to get a 75 percent loan to value and borrow the entire amount. However, many lenders want to see you put your own money into the deal.

You can also suggest that the owner take out a second mortgage. Say, for example, that the only loan you can get is a 60 percent loan to

Using a Second Mortgage to Get In with $0 Down

Value or worth = $100,000
Seller wants sale price = $75,000
Bank will lend only 60 percent = $60,000 first mortgage
Seller takes a second mortgage = $15,000 for five years
$60,000 + $15,000 = $75,000 total

value because your credit isn't good. The seller wants $75,000 on the house worth $100,000. The bank will lend you only 60 percent of that amount, or $60,000. You could negotiate for the seller to take the $60,000 and sign a second mortgage behind the bank's first mortgage for $15,000—not in cash, but in a note signed by you. This is another way to borrow the funds without using your own money to buy a property.

Buy On Owner's Terms

Many savvy real estate investors and some knowledgeable homeowners know there is another source of funds for all of their real estate needs. Instead of going to a bank or mortgage company to borrow the money to buy a property, they go to the seller or owner of the property. That's right, the seller can act as your banker.

If you find a motivated seller who wants $100,000 for the property, you could borrow the $100,000 from a bank or just get it from the seller. If the property is free and clear (i.e., no liens on it), the seller can give you a new mortgage for $100,000, just as the bank would. Instead of paying the bank mortgage payments every month, you pay the seller. It's called buying real estate on *owner's terms*.

Robert's Tip

Always, always ask for owner's terms. Almost all sellers will say that they want cash. But obtaining owner's terms is still possible—if you can negotiate. If sellers demand cash from you, ask them, "Why? What are your plans for the cash?" If they need it to pay off a small debt, then ask what they are going to do with the remainder once the debt is paid. If they tell you they want to invest it, ask them what percentage they plan to make on their invested money. They may believe they can earn 6 to 8 percent. Your response to this is, "How would you like to pay off your debt and earn 9 to 10 percent with a very safe investment?"

This offer should interest them because it meets their needs—they just told you that. You can then offer $3,000 cash down with owner's terms for the balance over 20 or 30 years at 9 or 10 percent interest.

If you don't have good credit, this is the easiest way to get financing. Even if you do have good credit, you'll probably get a better deal using owner's terms.

If you hold a property for one year or more and pay all of your bills on time, a lender perceives your credit as less risky than before. Your credit scores will probably improve. That means after one year, you could get a 75 to 85 percent loan to value on the property and pay off the original seller.

Go to a mortgage broker this week and ask that broker to preapprove you for your own personal home loan and for an investment property. Find out about as many loan programs as possible, because you will probably be selling to both home buyers and investors. Then call three Realtors, three real estate investors, three closing attorneys, and a few title/escrow companies in your area. Start networking to find motivated sellers, buyers, and sources of funding (and be sure to add your contacts to your databases). Ask them for referrals and recommendations for good lenders. You may also want to affiliate with them as partners. Ask if they will pay you referral fees for finding deals. Try all of these ideas and follow your best leads.

CHAPTER 7

In a good negotiation, everybody wins something.
—GERARD NIERENBERG

Negotiating Deals and Making Offers

To get great deals on property and buy them without using your own money, you're wise to learn how to negotiate well. Often you can negotiate a no-money-down deal if you are willing to learn how and apply it to many transactions.

You can actually negotiate in all areas of a real estate transaction: price, terms, closing time, earnest money, contingencies, conditions. Negotiate for all of it. Most real estate investors and Realtors negotiate only on price. Learn to negotiate in many areas, using price as the beginning step.

Rule 1: Negotiate only with the decision maker.

Robert's Tip

Go out in the next 24 hours and negotiate for something. Remember, only negotiate with the decision maker. When you're at a restaurant, for example, ask for the manager and build rapport by chatting and start a dialogue like this:

"How long have you been working here?"

"I've been working here two years," the manager says.

"What a great restaurant; Cindy the waitress is awesome. It's our first time here. We're just wondering, do you sometimes do special things to get people to come back?"

"Yes, we do. There's a little discount or sometimes dessert. Do you want some dessert?"

"We'll take some dessert."

"I'll bring a piece of cheesecake."

"Well, since there are two of us, can you do any better?"

You might think this is funny and crazy, but if you go out and start practicing, you'll get better at asking. When you buy a car, you negotiate with the salesperson, who rarely can do any negotiating. The sales manager there might make all the decisions on the pricing of the car, but it's the finance manager who makes all the decisions on the financing of the car. Talk with the right decision maker, no matter what the situation. Remember, rarely in life does something work all the time. However, if you try these negotiating tactics many times, they will work some of the time.

Have you have ever gone to a restaurant and seen people yelling at the waitress? The food is no good, the chicken is cold, the fish is bad, and the poor waitress is about to cry. She wants to help, but what can she do? Nothing; she's not the decision maker. Then she goes to the manager and the manager comes over to your table. This manager is the person you should complain to . . . the person in charge. Negotiate on a property only with the people who control it and can make a decision. Ask them, "In whose name is the property? Is it yours? Are you the one who can make the ultimate decision to sell?"

Here's a good example of how a few well-selected words can bring in thousands of dollars as a result of skilled negotiations.

When you call on a house advertised at a price of $200,000, and if that's a good deal, many investors may just offer the listed price. Let's say the property is worth $280,000. The seller tells you it's worth $280,000, and it is. It is a great deal. Many investors would just accept that great deal and have $80,000 of potential profit. Not bad!

However, what if you ask, "Why are you selling?" What if they respond that the mortgage is $150,000 and it's going into foreclosure. The sellers need to pay off the debt—$150,000—plus they need $15,000 cash so they can move. Now you know that they may take $150,000 plus $15,000, or $165,000 instead of $200,000. That one question could possibly save you $35,000.

Then you ask, "Can you do any better? What is the least you would take?" What if they say, "Well, if you could get me $10,000 soon, I'll take it." You just saved or made another $5,000 by asking some key questions. Perhaps you are skeptical and think that this does not work. It definitely does not work if you do not try it! This is exactly what happened to a student of mine, Carl, in Atlanta. By asking those key questions, he saved or made an extra $40,000 on what he knew was already a good deal!

Find the Seller's Pain

In order to find and negotiate good deals where you might be able to get owner's terms, you must find the seller's pain (i.e., motivation) and deal with it. If they do not have any pain or motivation, then you can't help them and will not get a good deal.

Ask them the following questions:

"Why are you selling?"
"How long do you have to sell?"
"How did you come up with your price?"

If they request all cash, ask them why. What will they do with the cash? Why do they need it?

Be inquisitive like a four-year-old and ask why, why, why. You must discover their true motivation, desires, and fears in order to structure a creative solution that helps them and allows you to get good deals with good terms.

Remove Your Emotions

Learn how to walk away from negotiating to get what you want. The less you care, the more money you'll make, because if you're emotionally attached to one property, you won't be a good negotiator.

I learned that lesson when I worked on Wall Street and watched people trading hundreds of millions of dollars of options. It can be painful for traders to lose $5 million of their money or their firm's money or their clients' money. The only way they can do this work is to have no emotion and not care. From what I could see, most behaved like robots; they just analyzed the information and acted, because if they became emotional, their decision-making process became cloudy.

When you're making decisions, don't let emotions get in your way. The one who cares *less* is the one who usually wins. Remember, real estate investing is just numbers. Remove your emotions when you negotiate.

You can negotiate on all aspects of a real estate contract. Of course, you must negotiate on price. Always ask for terms or owner financing, and also negotiate on time to close, closing costs, and all of the aspects of your offers or contracts. These steps will help you make more money and use less of your own money to buy and profit from real estate.

In my standard buyer's contract, the contract I use when I offer to buy a property, the typed-in closing time is 90 days, not 30 days. You will not always get 90 days to close, but if it is in the contract, you may get it sometimes.

Close 90 Days Out

Most contracts in real estate say that closing must occur within 30 days. Try this instead: Set your closings for 90 days out through your standard buyer's contract.

Let's say you're able to get financing in 20 days or get a partner to come in and buy the property in 30 days or wholesale it to someone in 30 days. If you have 90 days to close on a $200,000 deal, but you can close in 25 days, it's time to renegotiate with the seller. Here's a possible dialogue:

"The closing is 90 days from now. It will be the beginning of April when you get your $200,000. Would you like that money a little sooner? In fact, would getting the money in the next three weeks help you?"

The seller says, "Yes, I could pay off my bills and move a little sooner."

A conversation like that gets sellers to visualize and mentally act out what they would do with the money. Then you finally ask this question:

Robert's Tip

Follow the example of my Wall Street firm and do a preliminary sale. You'd say, "I think this house is worth $300,000. The repair person told me it needs $10,000 in repairs. A buyer should take $220,000 for it once it's fixed up. If those numbers are correct, that smells like a good deal."

The lesson is to put an offer in *first* with a contingency, *then* do your due diligence. You might come back to the seller and say, "Both you and a repair person thought it would cost $10,000, but repairs are really going to be $50,000. Because it's so messed up, it's not worth $300,000. It's only worth $100,000." Do you get upset? No, you just renegotiate because the deal was misrepresented to you and the numbers weren't right. But if you do your preliminary homework right and the numbers look good, control it first and then study it. Remember, until you have a signed contract, you have nothing. Do not spend all of you time analyzing a property.

"If I were going to get you cold, hard cash in your pocket sooner, that would help you move sooner and pay off your debt, right?"

Always restate what the other person said and then ask, "Would you take less?" The response might be, "I really don't want to come down. But I tell you what, if you got that money to me quicker, I'd take $199,000."

You made $1,000 just by asking that question. If you're a good negotiator, you could even get the seller down to $195,000 and save another $5,000.

Time: Use It Wisely

Remember, you have only one asset in life: time. Please don't waste it agonizing or worrying. Your primary goal is to find a motivated seller, shoot out an offer on the seller's property, and find a way to control that property. That's what you need to focus on like a laser beam so you don't waste time as you travel on your road to riches.

If someone won't talk to you or negotiate on a deal or things aren't going right, your backup plan is to shoot an offer and move on. Maybe the seller says, "I'm not negotiating. I want $400,000. That's it." When that happens, don't take it personally; just keep on moving forward. Make a low offer and then go out and find more motivated sellers.

For most situations, I recommend shooting a low offer in writing and including a contingency clause stating the sale is contingent on the

---

Robert's Tip

In my first year as an investor, I looked at houses, talked to people, and stood outside the houses waiting for lightning to strike me and tell me to buy a certain property. I was scared to death and I made no offers, bought no real estate, and made no money. That approach is guaranteed to produce zero results for you. I know, I tried it for an entire year.

It's easy to become focused on looking at houses, talking to people, and studying a lot. Those things are all important to do, but it's best to take action that results in making offers. If you never make an offer, you'll never be a real estate investor.

---

buyer's inspection approval. If the seller signs your low offer, remember, you don't have to buy it; for now, you simply want to *control* that property. Having control gives you the right to inspect the home and make an assessment. Once you've seen the house, it could be so undesirable that you'll want to forget the deal altogether. The contingency clause allows you to get out of an desirable deal. Caution: Do not put offers in if you do not intend to close on them. However, do your research, put an offer in, and then verify everything. Too many people spend all of their time stricken with paralysis of analysis. Make offers now!

Be a Confident Player

To become a successful investor who can negotiate good deals and get property without using your own funds, negotiate from a position of power, control, and confidence. Adopt the mind-set that says, "I am finding great deals. I am successful. I have a lot of deals to look at."

When doing your real estate business, present yourself as one who is confident, busy, and successful.

That means, as an investor, you don't phone sellers and whine, "Please, I've got to find a deal; sell me a property. What will you take? Can you do any better? Something needs to happen. I need to get one deal, just one. Please help."

I compare this posturing to dating—and no one wants to date a whiner. Imagine if someone came up and said, "I haven't had a date in a couple of years; no one will ever call me back; I don't have any phone numbers; would you please just give me your number and maybe I can call you some day and we can go out."

Not impressive. Instead, people prefer to deal with others who are active. A friend of mine, Doug, is a master at psychology and persuasion. When he was single, he said, "Robert, do you want me to show you how to get every girl in this place to want to go out with me, dance with me, and ask for my phone number?" I said, "Doug, you know you're not that great-looking—it's not going to happen."

So we went to a bar in which 50 out of 100 people there were women. Doug walked in with a big smile on his face. He's not a good dresser or an overly good-looking guy (sorry, Doug—in fact, people say we look alike). But he approached the most beautiful girl in the bar first and started to chat.

"Hey, how ya doin'? My name's Doug? What's your name?"

"Susan."

"Susan, great to meet you. Hey, I'll be right back. . . ." and he spoke to another woman, saying, "Hey, I'm Doug. What's your name?"

"Judy."

"Judy, I'm Doug. . . ."

"Nice to meet you."

"Judy, do you like to dance?"

"You bet."

"Oh God, that's great. Hey, I'll see ya in a little bit. Okay?"

And he walks over to someone else and asks, "What's your name?"

"Sherri."

"Hey, Sherri, I'm Doug. How are you doing? Are you a student? What are you doing here? Oh great, that's good. Do you like to dance?"

"Sometimes."

"Me, too; not all the time. Hey, I'll be right back. Maybe we can dance later. I gotta go." Each time he talked to one of the women, he was smiling, confident, and enthusiastic.

All of a sudden, every woman (and even the guys) in the bar were talking with Doug and smiling and laughing. Then he went back to each one of the women and asked, "Hey, you want to dance? Great, let's dance." A few minutes later, he said, "I gotta go." Then he would dance with someone else. Before long, all the girls and guys were commenting, "This guy's dancing with all the women and everyone knows him; he's having a great time. I gotta know this guy." Soon they were saying, "Here's my number. Call me." They crowded around him to talk to him. He taught me about posturing.

Can you do what Doug did in your real estate circles? You simply call on some prospective deals and say, "I want to buy 10 properties this month and I'm calling on about 15 houses today. What have you got?" Not a whiner's statement at all. If sellers start pressing you or giving you a hard time, just say, "I gotta go; I've got 20 more houses to look at." Of course, you must always be honest, polite, and sincere, like Doug. If someone offered you 10 houses this month for $10 each, would you buy them? Of course.

In this business, we've got the newspaper to go through and the whole multiple listing service (MLS). Since you can't get to it all, you have to posture and tell prospective sellers what you're doing. Be honest and up front with them. But remember your goal: to write lots of offers, then sign a deal.

Robert's Tip

If you can't find a deal or you're having trouble getting started, just shoot out five offers a day. If you do that for six months, you can assume *something* is going to happen. But if you don't shoot out any offers and just bite your nails and get stressed out, nothing much will happen. That's guaranteed. Five offers a day keeps the blues away.

Use a One-Page Contract

I recommend using a simple, one-page contract to make your offers. Your offer contract spells out the terms, protects your interests, and includes necessary disclosures and contingencies.

Especially if the seller is motivated and under stress, you don't want to add any confusion by using a complicated, 20-page contract or offer. Of course, in some states you need a longer contract to buy something, but I still like to keep things simple. If someone is a crook, you could sign a 5,000-page contract and still get ripped off. If someone is honest, you can make a deal happen on just a handshake.

When I worked for a major Wall Street firm, I learned a lot from how companies did their contracts when they'd buy and sell other companies. On one occasion, the firm I worked for was going to buy a $300 million company. To start the ball rolling, representatives from my company simply wrote a letter, which is called *intent to make an offer*. The letter said, "We want to buy your company for $300 million cash, and we'll close in six months contingent upon us doing our due diligence and approving of what we find." It also said this firm would have an exclusive right to buy the company for $300 million, called the *right of first refusal*. This means that up to the time of sale, the company can't entertain any other offers for the duration of the contract.

The prospective buyer certainly controlled that deal when the offer was signed. Only when the decision makers got signatures on that letter did they begin their due diligence. And the contract these big companies signed was one page; I saw it.

How to Make 100 Quick Offers a Week

Let's face it, once you have a one-page contract set up on your computer, you can create an offer in 30 minutes or less. One of my clients said, "Robert, I don't like to talk to people; I don't like to get out; I'm busy; I'm not a negotiator; I can't do any of this." When I asked if she could make offers, she said, "I have that one-page contract, and you showed us how to complete it with a contingency, so I could probably fill this out on my computer."

She realized it took only a minute or two to type an address and a price on a standard contract, print it, sign it, fold it, and put it in an envelope. So she began sending out 100 offers a week, which cost less than $40 a week (100 letters times the postage). If a house is listed in the multiple listing service (MLS) by a Realtor or advertised in a homes-for-sale magazine or listed in the newspaper for $1 million, she offers close to $500,000 but she uses odd numbers. For example, if a house lists for $1 million, she offers $482,316. If it's listed for $3 million, she offers $1,600,414. If it's listed for $200,000, she offers $99,413.

Every Friday, she tracks her activities: How many offers were sent? How many responses were received? Typically, she gets no response from 95 percent of the offers she sends out. Some respond and write things like, "I can't believe you offered $482,000 for this $1 million home; you're out of your mind! I hate you investors!" About 4 percent give that kind of a response, but the remaining 1 percent accept her offer or call back and say they can't sell for such a low price, but they are motivated. She then negotiates with the motivated sellers, which has led to the purchase of a lot of properties. Of course, she has a contingency clause in all of her contracts so that if the contract is signed she is not obligated to buy the property before she inspects and approves it.

By doing it this way, she gets between four and six deals a month and now owns more than 100 properties bought at 60 to 75 cents on the dollar. If you follow her lead and shoot out a lot of offers, you could make a lot of money, too.

Beginning investors usually want to do the due diligence part first. They want to find out everything about the house and the neighborhood and the plumbing and the carpet. They spend a lot of time before making an offer. By the time they get around to it, the motivated seller has already sold the house to someone else. Until you have a signed contract or an offer, you have nothing.

No Money Down: Difficult, Yet Possible

Here are nine ways to buy property with little or no money down.

1. *Negotiate owner's terms with the seller.* Try (and *always* try) to have the seller sell you the property with no money down, with payments to be made monthly.

Example: You find a home that you think is worth $75,000. You negotiate to buy it for $50,000, with zero cash at closing. The seller will pay all closing costs, and you pay $500 a month for 20 years. Sounds great, doesn't it? Well, *the seller would have to be pretty motivated to take a deal like this.* Nevertheless, I've seen it happen.

If the house needs work, explain to the seller that you are going to spend time and money repairing the house—which is like a down payment. Your time and your money are going into the house so that the seller has little risk. In the event that you do not make payments to the seller, the seller gets to take back a home that is much more valuable because you just fixed it up.

In negotiating owner's terms, always ask for the payments to begin as late as possible, with the first payment due in one year, in three months, or at the end of the first month. If you are buying to rent the house out, you can use the first month's rent to pay down your payments to the seller.

2. *Trade something you have of value.* This might be a car, a boat, tools. Barter anything you may have in place of a down payment. You never know what a seller might need.

3. *If the seller demands a down payment, ask the seller to agree to be paid on terms.* Example: Seller wants to sell for $100,000. You know it's a great deal, but you don't have the down payment. The seller insists on $10,000 down. Offer $11,000, but only if you can pay it over 30, 20, 10, or 5 years—or even 1 year.

4. *Borrow money from another source for your down payment.* Example: Credit lines, home equity lines, relatives, hard moneylenders credit cards (careful), life insurance policies.

5. *Use the real estate agent's commission.* If the seller wants 6 percent to 10 percent down at closing, negotiate with the agent to take the commission over time. At the closing, the seller generally has to pay the commission in cash to the agent. If the agent agrees (you'll be surprised at the agent's flexibility) to take the commission in the form of a note, this saves the seller some cash at closing, which can go toward your down payment.

6. *Assume the seller's obligations.* Instead of making a cash down payment, assume some of the seller's notes and/or obligations. Perhaps the seller has a payment due; offer to make the payment yourself as your down payment.

7. *If you are buying a group of properties or land, sell off part of the land/properties for more than you have optioned or contracted for.* Then take the proceeds from that sale and make a down payment. Example: You are buying four houses for $30,000 per house. You know that they

are worth more. You negotiate 60 days to close and you need 10 percent cash down to close. You flip one of the houses for $50,000 to someone else. At the simultaneous closing, you make your down payment from the $20,000 proceeds you just received on the flip. Yes, it can be done!

8. *Partner a deal.* If you find a property that is a great deal and you need 10 percent down to close (which you do not have), persuade a friend or an investor to partner with you. If your partner puts 10 percent down on the property, offer to split the profits 50-50 when you flip the house.

Example: you find an apartment building that is worth $250,000 for sale at $150,000. The seller wants 10 percent down and will carry a note for 20 years at 10 percent interest (approximate payments of $1,300 per month). The apartment building has 10 units, and each one will rent, on average, for about $450 per month (or $4,500 per month total). You can make $3,200 per month (before expenses, of course)! But you don't have the down payment. Tell a friend or an investor about the deal—ask for the $15,000 down payment and offer your friend a 50 percent partnership on the deal. In 10 months' time, your partner will recoup his or her down payment, and you'll be making $1,600 per month and building equity. And you didn't even put up a dime!

9. *If you can get a line of credit from the bank, use it to purchase property.* Use the equity in your home to obtain a down payment. You'll be able to pay off the down payment over time at a reasonable rate, and you'll have an interest reduction on your taxes.

CHAPTER 8

There are safe and unsafe ways of doing nearly anything. The knowledge or the knack of doing things safely is gained by experience, properly directed.
—RALPH BUDD

Dealing with Contracts

Spelling out agreements with legal contracts provides a safety net in real estate transactions.

Controlling the Property

You've found a motivated seller, made sure it's a good deal with room for profit, and you're ready to have the sellers sign a contract. Be sure to use a contract with one or two contingency clauses. For example, "This contract is contingent upon buyer's inspection and approval before closing." Then set your closing date on this deal, ideally between 60 and

120 days hence. Anytime in the next 60 to 120 days, you can inspect the property and say you don't approve, then tear the contract up. You don't have an *obligation* to buy the property or to close. You have made good use of this contingency clause. Of course, never sign a contract on a property that you do not fully intend to close on.

Another contingency clause could be worded this way: "Contingent upon buyer [insert your name] obtaining favorable financing based solely on the discretion of the buyer." If you don't get a 30-year loan at 2 percent, you could say the terms are not favorable and walk out. If someone says, "I'm not going to give you a contingency—inspect it now," then you'll have to make a business decision.

Be aware that some courts rule that a contingency clause can be too broad. They won't let it stand. If you're the one out of maybe 10 million who actually goes to court, it could get thrown out. Protect yourself by being specific (e.g., "contingent upon buyer's inspection and approval for repairs, repair costs, and marketability"), so that if your case is challenged in a court, you won't lose your investment.

Even when I'm sure I want to buy a certain property, I always set the stage for a way out. What if I win the lottery or move to Florida? What if I get out of real estate? What if the market changes? What if a bomb blows up in that city? Things happen, so limit your risk. There is no risk in having a contract with a contingency.

Some people are not trustworthy; they may sign a contract with you because they're motivated to sell. But if someone new comes along the next day and offers more money, the sellers might try to back out of your contract. Let's say that they close with the higher offer, but in the meantime, you've attracted a buyer and want to close on the property. The sellers surprise you by telling you it's already sold. To get your money—the profit you could have made or the property itself, you'd have to sue them, but they probably don't have money since they were motivated sellers to begin with.

To protect yourself against that possibility, go to the courthouse and file a copy of the contract or a letter against the property (called an *affidavit*). People who have interests in a property (such as loans and liens) do this. Say you file the affidavit the day after they sign the contract and they sell the property to someone else two days later. When they go to close on it, a title search is performed and they learn they can't sell the property because of your contract being filed on it. Consequently, they can't get valid title insurance and can't complete the deal. That's how to protect yourself when a real estate contract is broken.

Robert's Tip

If you need to file a copy of the contract or an affidavit stating your interest in the property, have your title company or attorney do the paperwork to ensure it complies with laws in the appropriate city and state. This reflects a decision *not* to become a title expert. You could learn how to do a search, how to file it, and so on, but knowing that won't help you make money. Your job is to buy and sell properties. It's like driving a car. Before you get into it, you don't need to know exactly how everything works. All you need to know is that you stick your key in it, pump in some gas, and go. If the car breaks down, you simply go to a professional who can fix it.

It's the same idea with real estate. Spend your time finding others who are experts in certain areas and hire them. You just need to use your key, turn it on, and go.

Dealing with Earnest Money

The Realtor or the buyer is going to want earnest money, or up-front money. Say you put down $10,000 earnest money on this contract and, three weeks into the deal or after the contract is signed, you do your inspection and say, "I don't want this deal; it's not going to work; the repairs are too much," and you walk away. What happens to your earnest money? You get it back because you have a contingency clause.

Here's another example: You buy a house and your contract says "contingent on getting favorable financing," but you don't get a loan. You had put down $1,000 in earnest money. What happens to the earnest money? You get it back.

You can get out of paying earnest money much of the time, so be prepared to make the best of it. Always ask this question of the seller or Realtor: "Who holds the earnest money?" Usually, the seller's brokerage company puts it in an earnest account, which is not allowed to earn interest. Or the seller holds it. You may protest, saying they're asking you to take your money out of your investments that earn interest and hold it in an account that doesn't earn any interest.

Let's put this in perspective. When we do hard moneylending, legally and ethically, we earn between 20 and 40 percent a year on the money we lend out. Taking the low end, that's about 2 percent a month. Make the argument to the seller's Realtor that you know ways to make 3 percent a month in real estate. If the seller pays you interest on your earnest money, you'll be more than glad to put it in that person's account. The seller will probably say no. Then it's up to you to you make it clear you're a serious investor and you don't put an offer in on a property that you aren't sure you'll close on. Also tell the Realtor you're looking at other properties and may want to work closely with him or her in the future. Then ask to be excluded from putting down earnest money on the current deal.

Produce an Identity Package

People don't immediately trust other people in real estate transactions; that's one of the reasons they ask for earnest money. To develop that trust, it's a good idea to produce a professional-looking identity package. Businesses have beautiful brochures with pictures of their CEOs standing by the big corporate headquarters. Sometimes the CEO is pictured shaking hands with the mayor or other important people. Its well-crafted language communicates that the corporation will help you and that it's okay to do business with them. You feel good about the company because of the impression left by its well-produced and persuasive brochure.

You, too, need a beautiful brochure. Spend some money on this; go to your copy shop and make an identity package with your name or your company's name on it. Think of a great name, such as International Real Estate Investors United. One of my company names is Superior Properties Corporation. That sounds impressive, doesn't it? It can sound big, yet have only two people in it. In fact, my nine-year-old son is a shareholder in my corporation.

Your identity package should contain the following:

- A photograph of yourself
- A resume

- Letters of recommendation
- Names of associates
- Testimonials
- Photos of properties you've sold
- Signed contracts
- Documents of closings you've done
- A list of activities you enjoy

If you don't have all of these because you're new and young, then gather letters of recommendation from teachers, Boy Scout leaders, ministers, rabbis, priests, and former employers. For your list of associates, put people on the board of your company to show you work with major Realtors and mortgage companies. Of course, you must get their permission to use their names in this way.

Every time you help a Realtor or motivated seller, have that person write a testimonial for you. It might say, "Jean was a great help; she did exactly what she said she was going to do. Thank you so much, Jean, for helping me sell my house. Sincerely, Maybelle Smith, October 1999, Columbus." "Jeff was a great help; he handled the transaction very professionally."

Your list of recreational activities will serve as possible connection points. "Oh, you like to fly-fish? I do, too." "You like to sail, play softball, ski . . . ? Oh that's great; so do I."

Keep this folder active by adding testimonials and photos and documents of your closings. It should get bigger every month. Whenever you go to the bank or are dealing with Realtors, potential sellers, lenders, buyers—anyone in your real estate circle—show them your identity

Impressing Others

A young man named Roger called one day and said he was closing a lot of deals. We didn't believe him, so Roger faxed over a closing document, a contract, another contract, another closing document, and a photocopy of a check. We were impressed.

Show others your contracts, your photos, your accomplishments. Then they will take you seriously and may not insist on getting earnest money. They'll want to find more deals for you because, obviously, you're a player; you're serious about being in this business.

package. Whenever you see potential sellers, pull out your folder to give them evidence of your experience.

If you follow my advice and put together a beautiful identity package, you'll be in the top 5 or 10 percent of all real estate investors. It will also help you convince Realtors that you're a serious investor and serve to give you credibility.

Buyer's Standard Contract

Put together a standard one-page contract that will work well for you. A sample contract follows and can also be found in the appendix.

Your contract should include the following components:

Title
On the top of the page, it says Standard Contract or Standard Agreement. It doesn't just say *agreement,* it says *standard.* Whose standard? Yours.

Beginning paragraph

"I _____ [your name] am going to purchase _____ property for _____ with the following terms _____, _____, _____. The property is a house located in _____ (city), _____ (state), _____ (county)." Include the seller's name and the date.

Body

"This closing shall take place in 120 days." (You could put 90 days or a year or whatever.) Once the contract is signed, you have this period of time to close. If sellers object to giving you 120 days to close, tell them to look at the top of the contract; explain that it's your standard. Of course, never let a contract get in the way of making money. If it's a great deal and they insist on a shorter closing time, you may want to do it.

Contingency

"This contract is contingent upon buyer's inspection and approval for marketability, repairs, and market conditions."

Assignable

"This contract is assignable." This means you can assign it to anybody, for example, you can assign it to the buyer you are wholesaling it to.

Seller pays all fees

"The seller shall pay all closing costs, including but not limited to, attorney's fees and title insurance."

Access to property

In the contract, also write (under conditions or extras or appendices) that you have the right to show the property, because you are going to show it to many people. You might also want to put in writing that you may show the property to your appraisers, your partners, your finance

Why State "120 Days to Close" as Standard?

You want to have 120 days to close for three reasons: (1) It will take the pressure off to sell it quickly; (2) it will give you time to find a buyer; (3) it's an effective negotiating tactic.

Say a home is worth $300,000 and you've got it under contract for $200,000. You have a buyer lined up to pay $230,000, so you'll make $30,000. But she's ready to buy it next week, not at the end of 120 days. She's a cash buyer; she has verified the funds to close; you've got a copy of her bank statement; you're ready to go to closing, too. At that point, go back to the seller and negotiate. Ask him, "If you had the money in your hands sooner, what would you do with it? What is the least you would take if you can get that cash in your hands three weeks from now?" Chances are, he'll take $185,000. That means you would make an extra $15,000. However, you respond by saying, "Can you do any better? What is the least you would take? Can you do any better? Can you do any better? Can you do any better?" If he says $184,000, you just made another $1,000 profit. Then you would re-sign your contract, scratch out $200,000 and put $184,000, and go to closing. You just made an extra $16,000, using cash and time as your tools for profit.

Why State "Seller Pays All Closing Costs" as a Standard?

How did I learn this one? When I went to a closing years ago and looked carefully at the closing statement, I realized I was paying for everything. I asked why was I paying for everything, and the seller told me to look at the contract. I hadn't read it; I didn't pay attention to it, but I had already signed it. I realized I had agreed to something I wasn't aware of. Most people do that. So I decided to put that in my contract. However, I always make sure people read my contracts and understand the terms in them.

people, your insurance agent, and so on. You are always showing the property to somebody: Just get written permission to do it.

Your contract should also have the price, the terms, and words to the effect that the seller has the risk of loss until closing and that possession shall be given on the date of deed.

End

On the bottom, include a *B* because this is your contract to buy—your Buyer's contract.

Sample Buyer's Contract

When you are buying property, here's a sample contract for you to review, revise, and use in your real estate investing business. (You can also find this in the appendix.)

STANDARD CONTRACT TO PURCHASE REAL ESTATE
(from Buyer)

1. I/we offer to purchase from Seller the following described real estate, together with all improvements thereon and all appurtenant rights, located at:
   Address: _____ City: _____
   County: _____ State: _____ Zip: _____

2. The purchase price is to be $_____, payable as follows: _____ down and the balance over _____ years at _____%, payable monthly

3. The conditions of the Purchase are as follows:

    a. Subject to review, inspection, and written approval of my financial partner.

    b. Purchaser shall have the right to assign his/her interest in this contract prior to escrow.

    c. Seller agrees to allow purchaser to show property to prospective partners and clients prior to closing.

4. Is there an Addendum to this contract?
   Yes _____ No _____

5. Is this deal "All cash" or "Terms"?
   All cash _____ Terms _____

6. Possession is to be given on or before _____

7. Seller agrees to pay all Taxes and Assessments up to and including the month of _____, 200____.

8. All closing costs and attorney's fees shall be paid by Seller.

9. Closing date shall be 90 days from the date of this agreement, with title to the above-described real estate to be conveyed by Warranty Deed with release of dower. Title is to be free, clear, and unencumbered, free of building orders, subject to zoning regulations of record, and except easements and restrictions of record. The Seller shall pay for and produce a valid title insurance policy protecting the Purchaser at closing.

10. This offer, when accepted, comprises the entire agreement of Purchaser and Seller, and it is agreed that no other representation or agreements have been made or relied upon.

11. This offer is to remain open for acceptance until _____.
    Date: _____ Date: _____
    Seller _____ Purchaser _____
    Seller _____ Purchaser _____

THINK ABOUT IT

Please have all of your contracts and agreements reviewed and approved by a local attorney. Every state has different laws. Remember, your job is to make money in real estate, not to become a real estate attorney. Go to www.prepaidlegal.com/info/shemin and consider working with your local Pre-Paid Legal Services, Inc. attorney.

Seller understands by signing this agreement that the Buyer is a real estate investor and may resell the property for a profit. Seller understands and agrees that the Buyer does not represent the Seller's interest.

Seller's Standard Contract

Someone offers you $250,000 for a property that's worth over $300,000, and you get a contract on it. In one hand, you have a contract to buy that same property for $200,000 and, in the other, a contract to sell it for $250,000. You need a standard contract for the sale. It's similar to the buyer's contract at the top; at the bottom is the letter *S,* meaning it's your contract to sell. Here are some key components.

Title
On the top of the page, it says Standard Contract or Standard Agreement.

No contingencies
One line states, "There are no contingencies."

Earnest money

There is a big space for writing in earnest money. (I don't even have earnest money in the standard buyer's contract. Most of the time they forget about it.) On a $250,000 offer, there should be at least $25,000 earnest money, or 10 percent.

Closing costs

"The buyer will pay all closing costs, including but not limited to title insurance, attorney's fees, recording fees."

10 days to close

If the buyer has been preapproved, then all you need is an appraisal. That takes a week, so the seller's contract says, "You have 10 days to close." If the buyer doesn't close in that period, the earnest money is forfeited.

End

On the bottom, include an *S,* because this is your contract to sell—your Seller's contract.

Sample Seller's Contract

When you're selling property, here's a sample contract for purchasing real estate. Review, revise, and use it in your real estate investing business. (You can also find this sample contract in the appendix.)

Robert's Tip

Stress the urgency of closing the deal in a short time and explain that other buyers are lined up. By keeping the buyer on a short leash, if it doesn't work out, you still have time to find another one. Never say anything that is not true, but if you are doing your job, you will have other buyers.

STANDARD CONTRACT TO PURCHASE REAL ESTATE
(from Seller)

1. I/we offer to purchase from Seller the following described real estate, together with all improvements thereon and all appurtenant rights, located at:

   Address: _____ City: _____
   County: _____ State: _____ Zip: _____

2. The purchase price is to be $_____, payable as follows:

3. The conditions of the Purchase are as follows: Sold "As is"

4. Is this deal "All cash" or "Terms"? All cash _____
   Terms _____

5. Possession is to be given on or before _____ (date of deed).

6. Seller agrees to pay all Taxes and Assessments up to and including the month of _____, 200_____.

7. All closing costs and attorney's fees shall be paid by Purchaser.

8. Nonrefundable earnest money of _____ to be held by Seller.

9. Closing date shall be on or before _____, 200_____, with title to the above-described real estate to be conveyed by Warranty Deed with release of dower.

10. This offer, when accepted, comprises the entire agreement of Purchaser and Seller, and it is agreed that no other representation or agreements have been made or relied upon.

11. This sale shall close by _____.

    Date: _____ Date: _____
    Seller _____ Purchaser _____
    Seller _____ Purchaser _____

Disclaimer: The Purchaser understands and agrees by signing that the Seller does not represent the Buyers or their interests. This sale is contingent upon the Buyers being able to pass good title, which they may or may not have at this time.

CHAPTER 9

The opportunities of man are limited only by his imagination. But so few have imagination that there are 10 thousand fiddlers to one composer.
—CHARLES F. KETTERING

Using Other People's Ideas, Time, Money, and Credit

You're trying to develop all the ways to make money in real estate. How do you find them? How do you contract them? How do you lease-option? How do you do all this? How much time does it take to reinvent the wheel?

If you're like I was when I started in real estate, then you're busy over-analyzing, doubting, worrying, and wondering: "Does this really work?" You think, "Surely I cannot buy property without using my own money or credit!" You are trying (as I did) to reinvent real estate investing from scratch. I commend you for reading this book and educating yourself. Whether you think this is a great book or not, I guarantee that even if you use just one of the hundreds of ideas presented, you'll make a lot of money. Keep educating yourself. Learn. And use other people's ideas (OPI).

To find out more about courses, workshops, and other ideas offered, call my office at 888-302-8018.

Other People's Ideas

You do not have to create or reinvent successful real estate investing. You're better off finding other successful people who've learned what you want to know and using their ideas. That's why you have coaches and mentors. It's called other people's ideas (OPI). In 2002, I spent about $50,000 consulting with successful investors and learning just a few of the things they do. I'm using their ideas instead of trying to reinvent everything. Even though I am a successful investor, I am always trying to learn from others and improve.

Other successful businesses do that, too. Bill Gates didn't write the operating systems for Microsoft. He went to IBM and said, "If we had this operating system I envision, what would you pay for it?" When the decision makers showed interest, he wrote a contract for them to buy the yet-to-be-created operating system for about $1 million plus a few dollars for every computer that used it. What he did was controversial. In fact, three of his partners walked out of the meeting and told Bill he was crazy. But, really, he was smart. He did what's called a *reverse flip*—he found the buyer before he found the product. Then he went back to his home in Seattle, found a programmer, and paid the programmer about $50,000 to write the operating system. Then he took that contract and wholesaled the information to IBM—and others. He used OPI to great effect.

Other People's Time

How many deals can you look at in a week? How much bookkeeping can you do? How many properties can you fix? How many buyers can you find? How many deals can you fund?

Let's face it, you're limited by time. But you can get other people to use their time. For example, I have about 40 people looking for deals for me right now. (It should be 100, but I'm lazy sometimes.) Instead of looking for deals by yourself, instead of doing your own bookkeeping and financing, use other people's time.

Other People's Money and Credit

You have a choice: When you start your real estate investing business, you can use all of your own money and all of your own credit to buy properties. However, the most successful investors in the United States, those who own lots of property and make 10 times more money than other investors, never use *one penny* of their own money or *one point* of their own credit.

I recommend using other people's money (OPM) and other people's credit (OPC) because you can reduce your risk to almost zero.

Here are some ways you can accomplish this.

Funding Partners

When you do any business, know what you're good at, what you have, and what you do not have. Then you can find others who have what you don't have. For instance, I can't type so I don't try to type; I find a typist whom I pay to type for me. Similarly, if you don't have any money or credit, find people who do. They need what you have: the energy, the time, and the information to find good deals.

Bill Gates certainly didn't fund all the start-up costs of Microsoft. He asked seven people to lend him about $50,000 each to get his company up and running. Some of them told him, "This computer stuff won't work." However, five of them kicked in $50,000 each. Now some of them are on the list of the 100 richest people in the world, according to *Forbes* magazine.

You can do the same by forming a limited liability company (LLC) with others interested in investing. They could be uncles, aunts, wealthy friends, attorneys, accountants, employers, retirees—select people you trust and want to work with. You could find the deals and do the leg-work; they could fund the deals and benefit from the tax advantages available through real estate. (As you set up your partnership, be sure to claim at least 51 percent ownership—even 70 or 80 percent—so you can keep the majority of control needed.)

A successful investor I know in Florida owns 300 houses. He either puts them in an LLC or in the name of his partners—those who borrowed the money to buy these houses. This investor owns 60 percent of the properties. He makes all the decisions about managing them and when to sell them. This arrangement allows his partners to build their wealth as the tenants pay off the debt or the houses. Each month there is positive cash flow, and when the houses are sold, everyone profits.

Here is how he does it. Using many of the techniques in this book to find deals, negotiate, and so on, he locates a likely property. For instance, he found a house in Florida worth $150,000. It needed $10,000 in repairs, and he negotiated a price of $99,000 because the seller was motivated. With repairs, he needed $109,000 to buy the house worth $150,000. He joined forces with a wealthy businessman who had just lost a lot of money in the stock market and wanted to get into real estate. The wealthy businessman was easily able to borrow $120,000 on the $150,000 house, because he had great credit and excellent banking connections. The house is titled to a limited liability company (LLC), with my friend owning 60 percent and the wealthy borrower owning 40 percent. All of the agreements and disclosures are in writing.

My friend received $5,000 up front for finding the deal. The excess $6,000 (they had borrowed $120,000, but needed only $109,000, minus the $5,000) went into a resource account for any expenses. They lease-optioned the house for $1,400 a month. The note, taxes, and insurance were about $1,000 a month. The wealthy borrower gets most of the depreciation of the house as a write-off against his taxable income. Each month these partners split the cash flow after the expenses are paid 60-40.

The tenant-buyer bought the house in one year for $155,000 (it had appreciated). At the sale, the bank debt was paid off first, $120,000. Then the profit of about $35,000 was split 60-40. My friend made $5,000 up front plus 60 percent of $35,000, or $21,000, at the time of sale. The wealthy investor realized his goal of investing in real estate, took some write-offs, generated cash flow each month, and earned about 40 percent of $35,000, or about $13,400.

The wealthy investor did not use any of his own cash, only his credit. He borrowed the entire $120,000 for the house. My friend did not use his own money or credit and made a lot of money. Of course, like him, you must find a good deal that is a win-win situation. You must make sure the numbers are good and get a good attorney to do the paperwork. Your job is to find good deals and good sources of funds and credit to finance your real estate business.

Support Team

Start assembling your team now so they're in place when you expand your real estate investing business. Get mortgage brokers and bankers on your team and tell them your plan (e.g., to do one deal a month or one deal a year or 20 deals a year; to buy and rehab 30 houses a year; to wholesale one property a month). Once you've made your plan, show it to them and say, "I'd like to work with you, and we can both profit. I'll send you business and we can work together."

In addition to a mortgage broker, you'll need a real estate agent, an appraiser, a property manager, other successful investors, and two or three good referred contractors (because you'll need to do repairs on your properties).

To find good people for your support team, go to meetings of your local real estate association or your local apartment association and ask people these questions:

- "Who's a good mortgage broker? Who do you use?"
- "Who's a good property manager?"
- "Who is a good mortgage broker and gets the deals done?"
- "Who's a good real estate attorney?"
- "Which closing company or title company do you recommend?"
- "Which contractors do you recommend?"

Go to my web site, www.robertshemin.com, to get a list of real estate associations and referrals for good loans and attorneys.

Once you've gathered names and phone numbers of people referred to you, sit down and talk with these referrals. Maybe even take them to lunch. They'll help you do business and answer your questions, too. Make arrangements to either pay them for their time or refer business to them in exchange for their help. When your sister wants to buy a house, speak up and say, "I know a good mortgage broker. I know a good title person." You may even get part of the commission for the referral. Because they're making money from your contacts, they'll be happy to help your business and answer your questions.

You'll quickly see how developing good relationships with these key people fuels your business because they know potential sellers, motivated sellers, property managers, mortgage bankers, Realtors, and potential buyers. Make them part of your inner circle, your board of directors, your team, your advisory counsel.

In fact, set up a plan. Every week, interview people and add one more really good member to your real estate investment team. As you do, you'll learn a tremendous amount. You'll find deals and buyers and money. And your belief in yourself will go up with every referral they send your way!

Start building your team now. In order to be a successful real estate investor and buy property without using your own money, you must have a team. Start to build your business now.

Identifying Your Team Worksheet

Find three good Realtors who can help you find good deals, run comparable sales, and sell some of your good deals. List them here:

_____   _____   _____

Find three good real estate attorneys and a title company that can help you with contracts, closings, and business referrals. List them here:

_____   _____   _____

Find three great mortgage brokers to help you and your clients fund purchases. List them here:

_____   _____   _____

Identify a great real estate accountant who deals with real estate investing. List that person here:

_____

Locate five money partners to help you fund your deals. List them here:

_____   _____   _____

_____   _____

Select two hard moneylenders who make loans on properties (do some networking at local real estate meetings or look in the newspaper). List them here:

_____   _____

Find seven serious real estate investors who are actively buying properties. You can find them at your real estate meeting, in the newspaper, or at auctions. You can wholesale properties to them. List them here:

_____   _____   _____

_____   _____   _____

_____

Choose three good, referred, licensed contractors or handy people who can help you and your clients repair properties and do repair bids. List them here:

_____   _____   _____

Find two older, perhaps retired, successful businesspeople to consult with you on your general business plans, policies, and procedures. Some cities have a SCORE group. (SCORE is an acronym for Service Corp of Retired Executives, a nonprofit organization with chapters across the country.) Call a large bank or the Small Business Administration for a referral to a local SCORE group, retired executives, and businesspeople who can help you for a small fee or for free. List them here:

_____   _____

Take a few successful real estate investors to lunch once a week. Ask them how they find deals, how they fund them, and what you can to do help them.

Lunch partners:

Week 1 _____

Week 2 _____

Week 3 _____

Week 4 _____

Week 5 _____

Week 6 _____

Week 7 _____

Week 8 _____

Should Investors Be Realtors, Too?

What are the advantages and disadvantages of being a Realtor while being a real estate investor? Real estate investing and being a Realtor are two completely different businesses. However, if you do get your real estate license, there are advantages and some disadvantages.

You could sell property and earn a Realtor's commission, usually 6 to 7 percent of the sales price. You work in an office with access to the multiple listing service and to a computer, fax machine, and phone. You're around people who are buying and selling real estate and mortgage people, so you'll learn quickly.

But consider these disadvantages:

- Motivated sellers may not want to talk to you because they think you just want to list their house for sale if you are a Realtor.
- If anything goes wrong, you are held to a high professional standard. You may be blamed since you are a professional real estate agent operating under a lot of regulations and disclosure laws.
- There is tremendous regulation. You have to use your real estate company's contracts, disclosures, forms, and so on. In my businesses, I want as little regulation as possible.
- If you are a Realtor, you can't pay finder's fees to people who aren't Realtors, so when your repair person or postal carrier brings you the deal of the century and wants a finder's fee, you can't pay it. If you pay finder's fees to other Realtors, they will probably stop working for you if you don't pay them.
- It requires paying a lot of fees: monthly fees, access fees, license fees, education fees.

I gave up my real estate license because there were too many rules. Even though I wanted to follow them, I wasn't sure I was always in compliance

Continued

Should Investors Be Realtors, Too? *(Continued)*

because they were complicated. For instance, every time I talked to someone, I had to tell that person immediately that I was a Realtor. If I ran an ad, I had to put the Realtor's symbol in the ad or I'd be violating the rules. If I placed a For Rent sign on my own property, I'd have to put "Realtor" on the sign. There are so many rules and regulations, I decided to give it up.

Instead, I became part owner of a real estate brokerage. I wasn't a Realtor, but I did own part of the company, and when people made commissions I received part of them. You can own a brokerage and walk in the office and ask someone there to run the comps. Realtors can prove to be a big asset to investors, but they represent two completely different businesses. You must weigh the advantages and disadvantages of being a Realtor and/or being an investor.

Robert's Tips

Take your time to find people who behave ethically, because you want to refer only those who do really good business to team members. Any time you run into a roadblock, instead of worrying about it, all you have to do is pick up that phone and dial a few numbers to get the help or answers you need. For example, if you want to know how much a piece of property is worth in a particular part of town, call your Realtor friends and ask them to run comps. Similarly, if you have a problem with a contract or a title, call your title company or your closing agent to get the answer. They know all about those things. They're part of your support team and your overall system. Stop wondering, stop worrying—just call someone for help.

No Beauty in Being Big

When I was starting out, someone told me that he had hundreds of properties, dozens of employees, tons of overhead, and then he said, "Robert, I was so happy when I was like you. A couple of properties, time was my own, flipped a couple a month, made a bunch of money." Even though this gentleman had hundreds of thousands of dollars a month coming in, he had lots of expenses going out. There's no beauty in being big. You'd be better off doing one or two wholesale deals a month, signing one or two lease options, and taking three months off each year. That would put $100,000 to $300,000 in your pocket. Compare that to earning $1 million, spending $800,000 of it on overhead, and dealing with all the headaches of running a big business.

CHAPTER 10

Opportunities are swarming around us all the time, thicker than gnats at sun-down. We walk through a cloud of them.
—HENRY VAN DYKE

Finding and Evaluating Deals

The secret to your success in real estate is finding good deals and knowing how to evaluate them.

Ways to Find Deals

The following methods have been proven to work over and over again by my students and countless other successful real estate entrepreneurs. As with any business, real estate is a numbers game. To find good deals from motivated sellers, properties selling at 20 to 50 percent below what they are worth, you must be willing to talk to, look at, analyze, and negotiate with a lot of potential sellers. Purchasing with no money down takes patience and persistence. Currently, I look at about 40 to 80 potential deals to find two or three bargain properties so I to can eventually close on one. It is worth it. Say you can wholesale a property and make $8,000 in profit without using any of your own capital or credit. Basically, you're making $80 to look at a house, presuming you look at 100 houses to find one deal that earns $8,000 profit. Pick one, two, or three methods that you like to do, find good deals, and stick with your decision.

Here are some ways you can find deals in your area.

Business Cards and Flyers

Give your business card to everybody you meet. Create attention-getting flyers and cards in colors like pea green, yellow, or purple. You can even have them made up to look like $100 bills and fling them around. Here's a sample business card:

Cash for Your Property

Call Now 000-000-0000

Close Quickly

Earn $500 cash if I close on a house you told me about

Estate Sales   Divorce   Foreclosure   Need to Move

John Smith
www.Ibuyhouses.com

Here's a sample ad:

Call me first or call me last

CASH for your House

Call Now

000-000-0000

Jill Smith

www.Ibuyhouses.com

Buy Ads

A common way to get started is to place ads in the local papers where you're doing business.

I've spent a lot of money studying successful investors, including a guy in south Florida who has made $100,000 a month at real estate for the past two years. He took this information about running ads a step further. He spends about $10,000 a month, or $120,000 a year, running ads on TV. He appears on the ad himself and says, "I'll buy your house if you're getting divorced, need to move, or are having financial problems." The ads are a bit funny, but effective—they get attention and he runs them continually. He gives out a phone number and says he'll make an offer if you want to sell your house. He also puts up signs on

Gary's Success through Placing Ads

One of my most successful students is a guy named Gary. He was selling frozen food to grocery stores in Ohio when he came to my first seminar many years ago. Gary's a quiet guy who sat through two days of learning, went through all the materials, and at the end we sat down privately for a few minutes. Gary asked me, "Robert, I'm not a real sophisticated guy, and I have no real estate experience, but I'm a hard worker. You tell me what to do and I'll do it. If I work 40 hours a week, just like at a regular job, and do this stuff, how many deals do you think I could find a week?" I said, "If you work 40 hours, you ought to be able to at least find one." So Gary wrote on his plan, "I'm going to find one deal a week, and I'm going to either wholesale it or use other people's money to buy it, fix it, and sell it."

Gary's main motivation for doing real estate was to quit traveling with his job so he could see more of his wife and child during the week. He made about $42,000 a year at his job, but he was tired of spending nights in hotels away from his family, so he quit his job a week after he got home from the seminar.

Of all the ways to find deals, he liked running ads best. In his local newspaper for a city of about 300,000 people in Ohio, he ran ads offering to "buy your house. I'll make an offer, call me." Seven similar ads were in this paper, but even so, Gary's ad drew five to eight calls a week. He got one deal from his first 12 calls. The first year, his goal was to flip 52 properties, or about one a week. He didn't meet his goal; he flipped only 47. But he made over $200,000 during his first year. In his sixth year, Gary made about five times more money in real estate than I did that year!

Gary still finds most of his deals by running ads. He rehabs houses; he flips and lease-options them; and he is making a lot of money.

Gary has been a seminar participant who has done well as an investor. To find out about upcoming seminars, call 888-302-8018.

corners all over target neighborhoods. He gets permission to place the signs and you must do the same. *Make sure that it is legal for you to place signs.* He did a study and learned that people see his ad approximately 20 times before they call. From 100 to 150 calls a month, he gets 8 to 15 deals. Every month, he builds, builds, builds, and perfects his ads. He wholesales the properties and makes about $6,000 to $15,000 profit per house. He specializes in homes in the $60,000 to $100,000 price range. In his worst month last year, he made more than $60,000. His real estate profits fund the ads; he's never used any of his own money.

Billboards

A franchise company in the United States, called Homevestors, works with investors to find and market homes. When you give the company a franchise fee, its trainers show you how to run billboard advertising. Maybe you've seen Homevestor billboards. They say, "We buy ugly houses." I've met people with Homevestors who are making a lot of money every month because they are advertising.

Publicity

Send out a media release to local media outlets saying, "I'm trying to buy 100 houses." Run some ads in the newspaper with your phone number. Write down your action plan for running ads, the amount of your budget for that purpose, and how you can start finding some good deals.

Direct Mail

You can purchase a database of out-of-state property owners and send them direct mail fliers saying, "If you're an out-of-state owner and want to sell your house, I'll make an offer. I'll buy—cash." Expect a low response rate to direct mail; you have to send out a lot to get any response. But it can be worthwhile. Remember, if you call *and* send a letter, your response rate will triple.

Door Hangers

To publicize your business, have people place door hangers around the neighborhoods you select. A sample door hanger might say:

Cash for Your House

Will Make Offer!
Call 888-888-8888
Fees paid if you refer me to a house that I close on.
Earn $500!
Call Jill Smith

Signs

You might place signs on neighborhood corners, on park benches, on billboards—it all works. Also put a magnetic sign on your car saying "Cash for Your House. Call [your name] 888-8888." Every investor I

A Not-So-Tacky Sign

I once flew up to Ohio to meet with a big real estate investor. He picked me up at the airport in his Jeep, on the side of which was printed, "I buy houses for cash." I thought that was so tacky. He had a really nice Jeep with this stupid plastic sign stuck to the side. I asked him, "Dennis, this is kind of cheesy, man. We're both serious investors, but I wouldn't ride around in my nice car with a sign on the side. Why do you do this?" He said, "Robert, I get about a deal a month. I just made $12,000 on a deal that came to me this way. Is that a good return on that $80 stupid plastic cheesy sign stuck on the door?" I saw Dennis later, and he still has the sign—and he's still getting deals.

know who has a car sign finds at least a couple of great no-money-down deals a year this way.

Network Advertising and Referral Fees

Join other people who are advertising, doing door hangers, running ads. See if they'll let you piggyback and save some money. Instead of spending $1 for a mailing, find someone else who's spending $1 for a mailing and give that person money to include your material in his or her mailing. One of my students took this idea and put his ad on restaurant menus, and he landed some great deals.

Real Estate Agents

Which real estate agents do you want working for you? In any given neighborhood or city, there are hundreds of real estate agents. I know many are very professional and have great intentions. However, in most towns, only a few are selling a lot of houses. Find the most successful agents and get to know them. When I went to Miami, I looked to see who had the most listings for properties along the beach. One company had almost all the listings, so that's who I wanted to get to know. These are the players, the people who are active. They have buyers, listings, and potential motivated sellers.

Always pay them commissions when they help you. I love paying agents commissions. Realtors really *earn* their commissions. They drive buyers around all day, tell them about schools, meet them for lunch, show them pictures of many houses, and answer the silly questions that the sellers and buyers ask. It takes lots of time. Be sure to have two to four active real estate agents on your team. Some specialize in working with investors; get to know them, too. Beginning agents who are hungry for business can also be good. Tell them what you're looking for and get them to help you.

THINK ABOUT IT

Never, never, ever take advantage of someone. One of my main policies and procedures is that I will never do a real estate transaction that's not a win-win situation for all involved.

Make this your guiding principle also. If someone, including you, feels taken advantage of, then don't complete the deal. Make sure the transaction that offers you the property at a discount will solve the seller's problem, then go ahead. If you look hard enough, you'll find plenty of good deals, so never go for a bad one. What goes around comes around.

Attorneys

Get to know the attorneys who work with bankruptcy issues, divorces, estate sales, real estate, and foreclosures because you may be able to get referrals from them. Remember, though, they have confidentiality agreements with their clients and may not be able to share everything they know. However, their clients have properties for sale, and you may find some good deals from this source.

CPAs and Financial Planners

When people have financial problems, they go to their accountants and financial planners, and you should too. Many people ask their financial planners and accountants for advice when they're in financial trouble, getting divorced, or have to deal with an estate. Also, many older investors who own a lot of property want to liquidate, and their financial advisors might be able to lead you to these deals. Network with these professionals and let them know that you can buy their clients' property and help them solve their problems.

Administrators at Nursing Homes

Our population is getting older, and a lot of people are going into nursing homes. Generally, their family members live in other cities, states, or areas of the country. People who enter nursing homes may have a house that hasn't been fixed up in 20 years. Family members may ask the nursing home administrator what they can do with their loved one's property. "We've got to sell the house. Can you help us out?" Network with some nursing home administrators to see if they know of people you can help by taking over their houses.

Codes Court

I love courts because courts create tons of motivated sellers. Codes court disciplines people who have violated local codes regarding such things as trash or the disrepair of a home. To find out which homeowners have infractions and may be motivated to sell their homes, contact the codes department. The list is a matter of public record and you can usually get a copy of it.

Eviction Court

Have you ever been to eviction court? If you like crazy, wild stuff like on *Jerry Springer* and reality shows, eviction court is much better! Many tenants and landlords represent themselves in court. What surfaces is money, sex, intrigue, violence. It's wild.

Who finds themselves in eviction court? Landlords and property managers who haven't received their rent. The tenants probably tore up their property. You'll find some highly motivated sellers there. I sit in the back and just record everybody's name as they're leaving and/or talk to them out in the hallway. I ask, "Do you want to sell your property? Are you tired of tenants?"

By the way, if you don't like to talk to people in the back of the eviction courtroom like I do, you'll find their names, addresses, and/or their

Dale's Success Story

One of my seminar students is a guy named Dale. He said, "I'm really busy, but I want to do this real estate thing. I can get a list of code violations in Tennessee. In one of the towns, there's a list every month of 80 to 150 properties with code violations." Dale finds the owners' addresses, which are on the codes list, sends owners a letter saying he'll buy their houses, and follows up with a phone call. The sellers may say, "I've got to fix this stuff; the codes court is all over me. What can I do?" Dale replies, "Would you like me to buy your property?" He does some research with the codes department to make sure the house isn't scheduled to be bulldozed that week. He asks the officials there if they'll give him a permit to fix the house if he buys it. Usually, they say, "Yes, but you don't have a lot of time." So he puts an offer on the house. If it's worth $100,000 but needs $20,000 of work, Dale may offer $20,000 or $30,000. Then he runs an ad in the newspaper saying "fixer-upper handyman special." People who like to buy houses, fix them, and sell them usually respond. He shows the house to all callers at the same time and finds a buyer that way. He made $12,000 on the first house he wholesaled by selling it to a rehabber.

Selling one house a month this way, Dale made more than $100,000 in his first year as a part-time investor. He didn't use any of his own money. He found a motivated seller, did his homework, and put in an offer. His accepted offer didn't have to close for 90 days. He ran ads and built a network of buyers of distressed properties. He didn't buy the homes, or own them, or borrow money, or deal with repairs. He just wholesaled them. Now Dale is a full-time investor and uses the cash he made from wholesaling to buy houses. He's still not using his own money: He *created* the money by beginning with wholesaling.

attorneys' names on the docket, usually posted on the wall outside the courtroom. Get names, write letters, and make phone calls. I've been teaching this for about two years now, and I still don't know hardly anyone besides me who's doing it. Yet every time I go to eviction court, I get a deal.

Divorce Court

The records for divorce court are a matter of public record; generally, you can look in the files and see the assets of a divorced couple. I urge you to spend about three or four hours in your local courthouse and look in the divorce records. Then send letters, make phone calls, and submit offers. If you do that repeatedly and get to know people at the courthouse, you'll probably find some deals.

Estate and Probate Court

A lot of times, people who die owned homes or other types of property that their families simply don't want. Here's an example of creative deal making.

Obituaries Lead to Sales

One of my students writes a letter and calls on every obituary in the newspaper before the estate goes to probate court. He is only part-time, but has lease-optioned or acquired owner's terms from the estate for no money down on four houses in only two months. The equity in these properties totaled over $250,000. He put zero down, made payments to the families, and lease-optioned the homes to tenant-buyers. It may seem dark and morbid to call on obituaries, but he is all the richer for it. Surprisingly, the families have all been appreciative that he took the real estate off their hands.

Environmental Court

If you have trash in your yard or your grass gets too high, the environmental or health department in your community could send you a note, fine you, or put a lien against your house and take you to court. As an investor, you want to go to those courts and talk to the players, because you'll find motivated sellers who could pay big fines if they don't fix their property.

I was once at my local codes court when the judge said to a defendant, "You've been in here two times and haven't fixed your house, so you need to sell it or I'm going to put you in jail." I stood up in the courtroom and said, "I'll buy it." The judge told him to meet with me and sell the house because he had violated a lot of codes and health department regulations. The judge was happy that the man sold his house; the defendant was happy to sell to me so he would not keep getting hassled by the court; and I got a smoking great deal.

Real Estate Association

Investigate the National Association of Real Estate Investors. It has a list of all the real estate associations located in almost every major town. Associations are great because their members are investors, landlords, landladies, mortgage lenders, and closing attorneys. Also check out my web site at www.shemin.com, or call 888-302-8018 for a list of real estate associations around the United States.

Other Investors and Landlords

You find these people through real estate associations and through "I buy houses" ads. If they say "we loan money on real estate" or "we buy houses," call them, because they're now your favorite people. Sometimes they may find more deals than they know what to do with and will pass some on to you. In return, you can pass some on to them. As a matter of fact, I'd say 80 to 90 percent of all the wholesale deals I do are with other investors. They make it possible to do double and triple flips if there's enough margin in the deals. I suggest you network and meet people who are doing the business. Affiliate yourself with the good ones and your business will grow.

Tracking Worksheet

Keep track of your efforts in your quest to acquire property without using your own funds. Add to this form every day, week, and month to track your success.

Number of Leads	Sources of Lead	Offers Made	Number of Properties Closed	Potential Profit or Profit Made	Method Used (e.g., wholesaling, rental, lease option)	Profit per Lead

To determine your profit per lead, take the total amount of profit you made and divide that number by the number of leads looked at. For example, $10,000 profit ÷ 80 houses looked at = $125 per lead profit.

Intention Worksheet

My goal is to find _____ good deals a month. To do this, I must look at _____ properties. To find good deals, I will do the following activities daily/weekly:

1. Make _____ calls on ads in the paper.

2. Run an ad. My budget is _____.

3. Drive for dollars _____ hours.

4. Take at least one other investor to lunch each week.

5. Attend my real estate association meeting.

6. Meet with

   _____ Attorneys

   _____ Accountants

   _____ Mortgage brokers

   _____ Realtors

   _____ Financial planners

   _____ Others (specify) _____

7. Go to _____ court and try to find a list of _____.

8. Other (specify) _____

Review this intention list each day, week, and month to stay focused and constantly improve.

System for Analyzing Properties

Many people who want to be successful real estate investors and make money without using their own money never get started because they have paralysis of analysis. That is, they spend all of their time analyzing this business or that deal and never move forward. Once you find a potential deal or a motivated seller, there is a simple way to analyze almost any deal. Whether you're looking at a shack, house, duplex, apartment building, land, or strip mall, there are basically three numbers you need to know: (1) what the property is worth, (2) how much repairs will cost, and (3) what you can sell the property for. You must make sure that there is a 20 percent or greater profit margin based on these three numbers. Remove all emotion from analyzing your deals and just focus on the numbers.

To analyze any property, you need to know what the property is worth today by asking the seller, broker, or real estate agent. They know this by doing a valuation or fair market analysis (explained next).

Be sure to keep a folder on every property with the property's address on it. (For many years, I kept most of my property information on "stickies" underneath my car seat or on the back of envelopes. That's not a system. You must be methodical and organized.) In the folder, put the address on top, and include a property analysis sheet on which you have the name, address, phone number, how you found the property, names of others who may be involved, and so on. When you get answers to your questions, record them.

Valuation

To find out what a property is worth, you get three to five comparable recent sales—Realtors often call them *comps.* I always run three to five recent sales of similar properties on that street or in that area to make sure I'm comparing apples to apples. You can do it yourself by going to www.homegain.com or www.realtor.com. However, I prefer to have agents do it for me. I pay them for their time and refer a lot of business to them. Sometimes I get appraisers to professionally value properties. I pay them $100 to $150 to do a drive-by and run the comps on certain properties just to make sure.

Once you have comparable sales, verify them with someone who knows the market (e.g., Realtors or other investors). Call and say, "I've comped out that three-bedroom, two-bath house in that area at $350,000. I know that you sell or buy a lot of houses in that area—what do you think they are selling for today?" They may say, "Yes, some comparables will appraise at $350,000, but they sell for only $300,000." Or, conversely, "That neighborhood is hot! They're listing them for $350,000 and people are buying them for $400,000." Put those comparable sales in your property folder. If that property turns out to be a deal, people you show it to will want to see the comps. Or you may decide to keep the property and borrow the money from a bank, an associate, or a partner. The lender will want to know what's it worth, and the comps in your folder will help tell the story more professionally. Take the emotion out of your real estate and do deals by the verifiable numbers. Remember, always verify your comparables.

Repairs

The seller or the agent can tell you what repairs are needed and what they're going to cost, though sometimes they aren't as accurate as they could be. It's best to cover your interests and arrange for a written, detailed estimate from a contractor. If you plan to do the repairs yourself, be sure to include what your time is worth. For instance, beginners may say the property is worth $100,000, that they can get it for $80,000, and that they will do all of the repairs. They go on to say that it will take them six months to do the work. If they account for their time to do the repairs, they probably won't make any money. (You'd probably be better off looking for deals than doing repairs.) Remember to break down every repair bid by materials and labor and find out how long the job will take to do.

Sales Price

How much you pay for a property is a function of looking at a lot of deals, making a lot of offers, negotiating well, and finding and working with motivated sellers. To analyze any property, keep in mind these three key questions:

1. What is the property worth in today's market based on comparable sales?
2. How much will repairs cost?
3. How much can I, as an investor, sell it for?

Let's look at an example of buying a property to resell or flip.

When Rejected Offers Are Good

You do *not* want your first offer to be accepted, because you're gathering information. When your first offer is accepted, you offered too much. If sellers accept $2,000 a month for 100 months, that's $200,000, which tells you they might have taken $2,000 a month for 80 months. Instead of taking $200,000, they might have taken $160,000, but you'll never know. You don't have a chance to find out after they've accepted your first offer.

A friend of mine in Florida has done about 100 of these types of deals. Let's say the property is worth $200,000. He negotiates and offers to pay $150,000. The seller wants a small down payment. My friend carries an out-of-state check on a New York bank and writes the seller a $3,000 check if that's what he wants. (My friend negotiates very well!) The seller is happy because he has the cash in the form of a check, right then and there. He also carries a blank deed with him and fills it out at the kitchen table. He doesn't do contracts; he's never written a contract to buy a house. He just fills in the deed and writes, "I'll pay you $800 a month" (or whatever the terms are), and has the seller sign the deed. Now he owns the house. (If you write on a sheet of paper, "I [your name], do hereby deed to Robert Shemin the property at 123 Apple Street for $50,000" and sign and date it, I own that house.) My friend takes the deed, goes home, and calls his title company to do a title search to confirm that there are no liens on the property. Because he's written an out-of-state check, it takes a couple of days to clear. If the deal checks out, he lets the check go through; if not, he cancels the check and goes back and talks to the seller. It's that simple. He owns at least 100 properties. By the way, he got the $3,000 down payment from his financial partner of 15 years, who lends him the money at 10 percent. He's not using one penny of his own money, even though his net worth is more than $10 million.

An older three-bedroom, one-bath house in certain areas of Columbus, Ohio, might be worth $90,000 in today's market if it were fixed up. Say it needs $5,000 in repairs. The bank owns it and is asking $65,000. Your first offer of $45,836 was rejected.

That rejection says you need more information. The numbers indicate it could be an okay deal (because $65,000 plus $5,000, or $70,000, for a property that could be resold for $90,000 would produce a $20,000 profit). You want to buy it for $50,000. The bank wants $65,000; you may lose this deal over $15,000 and not make $20,000. Does it make sense to increase your offer if you can still make $20,000? If you won't go to $65,000, someone else will—someone who will spend $5,000 to fix it, sell it for $90,000, and make $20,000 net. Jump on it! You'll make plenty of money without being greedy. Get your offer signed quickly, because it's going to sell quickly.

Most investors buy property for one of two reasons:

1. To fix up and sell
2. To rent out for cash flow

Of course you now know some ways to profit without using your own money with wholesales, lease options, and creative finance. Always put yourself in the end user's place to make sure it's a good deal for everyone involved. If you're going to profit without using your own funds by wholesaling a property to a buyer who is going to fix it and sell it or rent it—run the numbers and make sure that it's a good deal for that person, too.

Generally, people who buy a property to fix it and sell it want to make at least $15,000 profit on a house that they will sell for $80,000 or less. On houses selling for from $80,000 to $300,000, they look for an 18 to 25 percent profit. Of course, these are just generalities. There are exceptions, but it must be worth the rehabber's time, effort, and cost to buy and fix a property.

Take the rent amount, then deduct mortgage, taxes, insurance, vacancy, and repairs. (Rent − taxes − insurance − vacancy + repair = cash flow.) Generally, vacancy and repair on a single-family home ranges from 15 to 30 percent of the gross rent. If the rent is $1,000 a month, take off anywhere from $200 to $300 a month for vacancy and repair. On a duplex, figure deducting from 25 to 40 percent for vacancy and repair, because duplexes are two-unit deals and people move in and out more frequently than for single-family homes. You'll have to incur costs for painting and renting them, and often they're empty longer than single-family homes, so you'll have holding costs, too. Some apartment buildings have a vacancy and repair rate of from 30 to 50 percent off the top.

Be sure to verify these estimates with property managers and Realtors in your area. That's something many investors forget about. If I plan to sell to investors, I want to make sure they can make money from the deal, and these numbers tell the story.

Take out the Emotion

Here's an example of how *not* to make an investment decision.

You look at a house and say, "Robert, I found a house. It's a great neighborhood. The people next door are nice; they've got a beautiful pool in the backyard, the kids are great, it's a really good school district." I ask one question: "What's the house worth?" "Well it's worth $200,000, but let me tell you about the stairs. They're really great." You go on and on with high emotion because you want to do your first deal.

I ask another question: "How much are the repairs?"

"Nothing, there aren't any."

Then I ask a third question: "What can you get it for?"

"They want $198,000."

"Wait a minute. You said it's worth $200,000, and they want $198,000. That's not a deal."

"But it's a great house. I love the neighborhood."

My suggestion is to get the excitement out of this transaction. All you need to know are the numbers. Unless you're going to live there yourself, remove your emotions from the process. Your investments are your investments. You're doing them to make a profit and to help people.

Determining a Good Deal

If a real estate agent says, "I have a shopping center for sale and the sellers are motivated," start negotiations by asking, "Why are they selling?"

"Well, they're getting out of the shopping center business and buying another business, so they need the money."

Does that mean they're motivated? Maybe. Ask more questions: "How long have they owned the shopping center?"

"Owned it for 30 years and bought it for $100,000."

"What's the current mortgage on it?"

"The property is worth $5 million and they just borrowed $4 million against it, so they owe $4 million."

Now you know. More than likely, the bottom price is $4 million, because that is what they owe.

"What's the least amount you think they'll take for this shopping center without negotiating? What's their rock-bottom price?"

"They want $5 million."

"What's the property worth?"

"Last year it appraised at $5 million."

Given this number, is that a deal? No.

"When do they have to sell it by?"

"Oh my God, they have to sell it in the next five or six weeks because a new deal's closing."

Robert's Tip

It doesn't matter whether it's a house, duplex, shopping center, or 100-acre land deal, get everything in writing. Don't believe what people tell you. Look at the comparable sales and keep them in your file for future consideration. If they're not motivated sellers right now, maintain the file and check back every two weeks or so, because things change. They could become motivated as time goes on.

That means they might be motivated, so you could offer $4 million and no more. If the sellers say yes, they can get out of the old debt and into their new project. You could put it under contract for $4 million and find someone to buy it for $4.5 million since it's worth $5 million. But that's still not a very good deal because the profit is thin and commercial property sales take longer than residential to close. Be realistic, and don't take a big risk on this. Remember, ask the questions, take out any emotion, and get the real numbers.

Property Analysis Form Worksheet

Address of property _____

Owner or seller's name _____

Phone # _____

Address _____

Type of property _____ Bed ____ Bath ____

How you found it _____

Referral name _____

Phone # _____

Address _____

Why are they selling it? _____

When must they sell it by? _____

Price wanted _____ Price negotiated _____

Value today _____

Repairs needed _____

Date purchased by owner _____ Purchase price _____

Amount of debt on property _____

Terms of the debt _____

Total amount of loan _____

Payments _____/month

Interest rate _____ Years left to pay _____

Title of paperwork is in whose name? _____

CHAPTER 11

Even when you're on the right track, you'll get run over if you just sit there.
—WILL ROGERS

Borrowing When You Have Bad Credit

Here's how you can get on the right track to borrow money even if your credit has been damaged.

Credit Repair

Credit repair is illegal the way most people present it. The only people who can legally and ethically repair your credit are yourself, a credit counseling service, and possibly your attorney. Credit repair is so important because it affects what you pay for money—for your cars, for your life insurance, for property. When you're buying property, it affects your ability to borrow. When you're selling property, your buyers' credit affects you. Half of all real estate contracts fail because the people can't qualify for financing, and knowing about credit repair will help not only you, but also your buyers.

I've had so many buyers who think they are unable buy a home because their credit is awful and they have no down payment. Then, 60 days later, they're buying a home because we helped them qualify for the down payment. We have also helped them increase their credit or use some creative financing techniques to take possession of the property. Let's go over some of these. This will help you buy and sell.

About half of all credit reports have a mistake in them, so you need to get a copy of *all* your credit reports. People can call credit companies and request copies of their credit reports. They're also available at www.shemin.com. Get a copy of yours and look it over. If there are mistakes, you need to write in and have those taken off. You can do that yourself, or you can hire an attorney or someone to represent you.

Challenge whatever bad information is in the report, and keep challenging it until it's removed. Under federal law, the credit reporting agencies have 30 days to respond, and sometimes they don't have the workers or the time to research and verify the information. If they can't do that within 30 days, they have to remove the offending words.

Understand that the law also says these companies don't have to react to frivolous claims, so there's a little leeway for them, but what often happens is that credit repair companies just keep challenging the facts (e.g., the date is wrong, the amount is wrong, this isn't mine). Simply for lack of people power, a bad rating may be softened. That's what so-called credit repair companies do—they keep challenging and challenging and challenging.

If an incorrect report isn't fixed, you have the right to request the original loan documents. A lot of people don't know that, and sometimes they can't produce them. That might also remove the credit problem. Certain bankruptcies are not reported accurately, and sometimes the bankruptcy courts don't respond when the credit repair companies call them to verify. Some people have told me that even bankruptcies may be removed just by challenging them. Again, credit rating companies don't have the time to respond. However, the challenges can't be frivolous. But who decides what's frivolous? A lot of people find that, just by challenging a report in writing, items are taken off.

You can do this yourself or you can get a professional to help you. Lots of credit repair companies say they can do it. Some of my buyers have tested one service that's actually run by attorneys. It's called www.CreditLawyer.com. I am not affiliated with them, but I've seen people get real results because they work with real attorneys. They're on the Internet, they charge $50 a month, and they usually work with people for three to five months. (Also, see the section about residual income in Chapter 2, "Systems for Success." It discusses a company called Pre-Paid Legal Services, Inc., which provides its members with attorneys who have achieved good results for some people because they know how to write effective letters.)

Get a copy of your credit report, check it, and challenge anything that's incorrect. Challenge anything you don't think should be on there and keep challenging. Make sure you do it with all three of the major credit bureaus, Equifax, Experian, and Trans Union.

Do things that improve your credit, and don't do things that hurt it. Be very careful about who checks your credit. When you lease or buy a car, sometimes the dealership sends out requests to eight or nine finance companies and checks your credit eight or nine times. All that activity knocks down your credit score. Ask everyone how they check your credit and how it will affect your credit score.

If you have a special situation that affects your ability to pay your bills (e.g., divorce or illness), you can write a nonemotional explanation, up to 100 words, and attach it to your credit report. Understand credit so you can help your potential buyers.

Money Brokering

We've discussed using other people's money. Now we're going to take it to the next level where it will become an entire business for you. Instead of borrowing money from the bank, you can *become* the bank. What do banks do? They take money in the form of deposits, paying 1 to 3 percent interest, then turn around and loan it out at 7 to 18 percent—and credit card companies charge up to 29 percent interest. Have you noticed that banks and insurance companies have the biggest buildings and the nicest lobbies? They do because they're taking your money, holding it, and lending it out. Stop letting the banks make all the money; you can learn to be the bank. You've learned how to analyze, verify, and find good deals. If a house is worth $300,000, it's a very low risk to buy it for $180,000. It's also low risk to lend $180,000 on something worth $300,000. Why? Because if people don't make their payments, you get something worth $300,000 for $180,000.

To broker money, use funds that are earning very little return in an IRA, a 401(k), or other investments. Roll them into a self-directed IRA, or do it directly and lend money to yourself.

By the way, your IRA cannot do "self-dealing"—that is, you can't lend your IRA money to yourself, but you can lend money on your own deals, or you can get other people to lend you money, and the rates of return can be rather high. You could use your own, but it's even better to use other people's money (OPM). Find people with a lot of money who aren't making much in their IRAs or 401(k)s or their investments, then offer them returns that are higher.

Start out by asking what kind of return they make now. If they make 7 percent, offer them 8 percent. If they make 8 percent, offer them 9 percent. If they make 10, offer them 11 percent, but don't go too high or you'll scare them away. So set up a business once you learn how to analyze property, then find other investors and offer to lend them money.

One of the biggest difficulties for investors who like to buy property to fix up and sell is that they're always out of cash. Even if you have good credit and a good business record, it's difficult to borrow money on a house that needs repairs. Yet most of the motivated sellers and good deals we find are on properties that need repairs. Half the roof is gone, or the floor has sunk, or the windows are missing. A person goes to the bank and says, "I'd like to borrow $50,000; the house is worth $80,000." Yet the bank or the mortgage company often won't lend money on houses that are in poor condition. They may *escrow* the money, but it's going to take 30 to 45 days to close because of all the paperwork, checking credit, gathering tax return information, and so on. Then, the week you're supposed to close, they might want more

---

Robert's Tip

Cash is king, quickness is queen. The more cash you have, the more deals you'll find. The quicker you're able to close, the more deals you'll complete and the more money you'll make.

---

paperwork. In the meantime, your motivated seller may disappear. You're better off to deal with cash.

One way to help people, including yourself, close more quickly is to have access to large amounts of hard money or private brokered money. Every state is different; check with your own state regulatory agencies to make sure you're not violating any rules or laws. If you borrow money at 8 percent, you lend it at 11 or 12 percent. At what interest rate would the bank lend to a real estate investor who has decent credit? Generally, between 6 and 8 percent, but rates change constantly.

A lot of hard moneylenders charge 5 to 10 points up front when the regular banks are charging 2 or 3 points, because the banks take a long time and may not close the loan. When banks are charging 9, 10, or 11 percent interest, a lot of hard moneylenders are charging 11 to 20 percent. Is that fair to the borrower? If the numbers work for the borrower, it is. If borrowers could lose a good deal otherwise, it is. Say they find a house that's worth $300,000 for $140,000. They're going to buy it, fix it up to sell it, and make over $100,000 after their repairs. For this to happen, the house has to close in two weeks, yet the bank said it's going to take a month to close and they may not even grant the loan because the house needs repairs. As a hard moneylender, you offer to charge them 10 points and 14 percent interest. Is that fair to those who are borrowing the money? Yes, because if they didn't have that money, they wouldn't be able to do the deal.

We tell people in the hard moneylending business that if you can go somewhere else or have the cash on hand, don't pay the extra points and higher interest rates. But most hard moneylenders are always low on money because there's so much demand. If someone would lend you money at 10 percent and you make 15 percent, how much do you actually make? Five percent. Five percent of $100,000 is $5,000. If you borrow the money and the lender doesn't charge you any points and you charge 10 points, that's $10,000. You've just made $15,000 by putting together the person who needs money with a person who has money.

Investors like you usually start out borrowing money, buying small properties, and renting them out. That works fine, but after a while, you get burned out dealing with the tenants. Then you graduate to the next level: buying houses, fixing them, and selling them, and that's great, too. You may make a lot of money and it works out well, but you're dealing with contractors, and the houses don't sell very quickly. You might be

Robert's Tip

What's one of the best ways to make money in real estate? Finance. Money. Paper. Because paper doesn't call and complain.

When you're a landlord or a landlady, tenants and the city call you all the time and bother you. When you're rehabbing properties, contractors call you to complain and cause you stress. If you're wholesaling property, you have to put people together, make sure the buyers can really buy, the sellers can really sell, and the closing really closes. It can be a headache. So one of the best businesses in real estate is paper.

making good money, but with lots of headaches. At this point, some investors graduate and learn that they can wholesale properties and make money just for finding good deals, so they start doing that. Then they learn about lease optioning and do that. Then, after 10 or 20 years in the business, if they're not either rich and retired or burned out, almost all investors get into paper. And you can, too.

CHAPTER 12

If a man has money, it is usually a sign, too,
that he knows how to take care of it.
—EDGAR WATSON HOWE

Protecting Your Assets

To jump-start your real estate investing without using your own money, protect what you do and will have. Many real estate beginners are scared to start investing because of the risk. With proper knowledge, correct disclosures and business practices, and an understanding of basic asset protection, you can and will be protected.

If you are sued and you've put assets in corporations, a lawyer could charge you with fraudulent conveyance. How do you defend against it? Show that you were solvent at the time of asset transfer when you made these corporations and trusts. Fill out a financial statement this week and sign and date it. You want it to show that you're solvent, that your assets are greater than your liabilities. If you don't do that and you are sued a year from now, it might be hard to prove. Put everything in writing and file it carefully.

Financial Solvency

Some of you have tried this asset protection program: No assets = no worries. But let's say you don't have any money and your insurance is inadequate and you're being sued. How would the lawyers collect the $800,000 (or millions of dollars) they think they deserve? They would wait until you got a job. Judgments are good for anywhere from 7 to 10 years in many states. Good lawyers might wait 10, 20, or even 30 years, hoping that you go to college, get a job, and make money. Then, whenever you have some money or a bank account or a house you want to purchase, they attach your assets. It's called *garnishment,* and it's similar to child support and alimony.

If you have money, who might come after you? Plaintiffs, lawyers, the government, the IRS, the EPA, the ex-spouse, upset business partners, or even clients. Start thinking about asset protection now even if you don't have any assets, because things can happen later. The following are ways you can start to protect your assets.

Avoid Risky Activities

You may think that sounds crazy, because it's just common sense. However, one of the most risky activities in real estate is property management. Managing tenants is the most sued profession in the world, even more so than doctors. You may want to stop landlording, which is what I did by setting up my friend in a management company. He wanted to become a property manager, so I helped him form a company, which he's proud to own. He follows my policy and procedures, but if the tenants are going to sue someone, they'd sue him, because he's the manager. He carries a lot of liability. Perhaps you, too, can hire a property management firm and pass on your liability.

Stop Making People Angry

Who sues other people? Angry people. The lady who spilled hot McDonald's coffee and burned herself went to the managers and said, "I have a dry-cleaning bill and I may have some medical bills. Will you

---

Robert's Tip

Look at the activities you're doing and see if you can pass them on to somebody else. For one thing, stop driving. That's a risky activity. I'm not a very good driver; I find it stressful and a waste of time, so I live in places where I don't have to drive. I walk, take cabs, and hire a driver.

I found an ad for someone who wanted to own his own limousine company, so I helped Limo John set up a limo company. He drives me around during the week as I go about my business. I sit in the back, talk on the phone, relax, and work. If I can make 10 more phone calls in a day and find one more deal, I've paid for the limo. He drives me around during the week, and on weekends he picks up bachelor parties, weddings, and prom-goers and charges $60 an hour. We split the money, so the limo company pays me. I make money and at the same time eliminate a risky activity.

---

do anything?" The McDonald's managers said no way, we don't want to hear about it. She became angry, then pursued her complaint on up the chain of command and got the same reaction. They didn't take care of it. She became angrier. It would have been a good policy to say, "Let's not make our customers angry." They could have paid her cleaning bill and offered her a couple of free Big Macs. She might not have been as angry. Instead, McDonald's chose to save some money and ended up with a multi-million-dollar lawsuit.

Most landlords, landladies, and real estate investors will try to save $200 by not fixing a commode or $50 by not meeting a tenant halfway—and then end up with a $500,000 lawsuit.

Stop doing things that could anger people angry; always work with them; be on their side. It's not worth it to make people angry and risk being sued. Weigh the real costs and benefits. Set policies and procedures and follow them.

Don't Have Employees

If you have employees, you're responsible for everything they do and everybody they run over. That's high liability. You can perhaps eliminate the risk of having employees. By making them subcontractors. Tell them to do whatever job they're doing, setting their own hours, following the subcontractor agreements, and becoming self-employed. I once had 18 employees who helped me manage my properties, did repairs, and so on. One day I made them all subcontractors. It was one of the best days of my life—reducing the headache and liability of having to manage employees.

Don't Do Repairs Yourself

If you repair something and it breaks and someone gets hurt, you'll probably be held responsible. One of my best friends in Nashville bought a house to fix up and sell. His contractor was repairing the deck, and my friend went out and helped him. He sawed wood, carried supplies, and helped nail part of the deck together. They built the deck, sold the house, and did a good job. The deck could safely hold 18 people. When the people who bought the house had a party, there were 30 people on the deck and it fell; 12 of them went to the hospital in an ambulance. They sued the contractor and won more than $1 million.

They also sued the owner. He called his insurance company, but his liability insurance didn't cover him for construction. He had been acting as a contractor without a contractor's or builder's insurance. Fortunately, he had implemented some of the asset protection tools you're about to learn. If he hadn't, they could have attached everything he owns personally, including his bank account. However, he had set things up properly in limited liability companies and some real trusts, and he negotiated a $3,000 settlement. Stop being a contractor; stop doing your own repairs. Pass that high-liability business on to the general contractor. Remember, you are responsible and may not be insured for all the activities you are tempted to engage in.

Stop Owning Things Yourself

That would protect you from being sued. One of my best friends owns more than 20,000 units of real estate and is worth a lot of money. Beyond that, he owns nothing. He drives a 1989 Honda Prelude owned by his company. LLCs and trusts own everything else. If you sue him, you probably won't get anything.

Tools for Asset Protection

Let's discuss a variety of ways you can protect your assets.

Umbrella Insurance Policy

I had a terrible car accident when I was a teenager. If my parents hadn't had any insurance on the car when I had this horrible wreck, they would have lost everything they owned: the house, the car, the bank account, the savings account. These assets would probably have been attached by the courts to pay for the judgment on the accident. Fortunately, my father had just paid an extra $140 a year for a $1 million umbrella policy, which protected us from losing everything.

I suggest you pull out your car insurance policies, real estate policies, and land policies, and read the exceptions. Property insurance usually doesn't cover nuclear war, terrorism, and mismanagement of city water. If the city floods and water ruins your house, your insurance probably doesn't cover it. Know your exceptions. For example, insurance doesn't cover you for any criminal charges. If you fall asleep at the wheel of your car and cause a wreck (or your teenager does) and somebody dies, you may be charged with manslaughter, and your car insurance would not pay for criminal defense. This a big hole in your asset protection plan.

Most likely, your car insurance agent told you $300,000 is standard coverage, and that's how much you have. But if you wipe out a family or put them in intensive care for three months, that $300,000 won't last long. Call your insurance agent and ask for details about a $1 million umbrella policy. It will likely cover your driving, possibly up to five rental properties, and other things. It's is a good policy that will probably cost only about $140 to $250 a year.

How an Umbrella Policy Works

Let's talk about how a lawsuit works. You're driving down the road and you get in a bad car wreck. You have only $100,000 of insurance, and the medical bills for the injured family are $500,000, plus they could get another $1 million if they sue you. You have only $100,000 in insurance, but you have a lot of real estate and money. Their lawyers immediately tie up all your property, saying you're about to be sued so you can't spend anything. They lock up your checking accounts while the lawsuit is going on. By the way, the IRS and other governmental agencies can also do that. You certainly can't operate easily if you can't use your bank accounts, can you?

Now let's say you have a $1 million umbrella policy. You injured someone in an accident, so you face a big lawsuit and the plaintiffs want a lot of money. Your insurance company calls them and says you have a $1 million policy. The company says it will write the plaintiffs a $1 million check. (Remember, their lawyer takes 20 to 50 percent of that $1 million.) The lawyer could recommend that his or her clients reject the offer and sue you, which could take three or four years in the courts. Winning in court may glean $2 million or more, but it's risky versus the likelihood of getting $1 million immediately. Under these circumstances, they'll probably settle out of court. You can see how an umbrella policy offers a lot of protection and could help avoid a lengthy, costly trial if something bad happens to you or your family.

Workers' Compensation Insurance

When you have people working on your property, make sure they have workers' compensation, and make sure you have a copy of the documentation. If you hire the same people every week, and if someone falls off your roof and gets hurt, you could be sued. However, you're going to say, "But the sign on their car and the words in their paperwork said licensed, bonded, insured." That doesn't mean they have any real insurance. If they don't have workers' comp, the judge might rule that the injured party qualifies as your employee and that you should have had workers' comp, so you might have to pay the $100,000 for a broken arm or a broken back. If they're doing only one job for you, however, they're not going to be deemed your employees.

In the appendix of this book you can find subcontractor agreements. Select one that works for you and make sure your subcontractors fill it

---

Robert's Tip

Get together with your insurance agents this week, discuss all your activities, and ask if you have enough insurance. If they say "absolutely," have them put it in writing. If they won't put it in writing, find another insurance agent.

One of my best friends was told $300,000 coverage would be enough for car insurance. She had a bad car accident, went to court, and lost a $950,000 lawsuit. On the stand, she testified that her insurance agent said she needed only $300,000. Her lawyer put the insurance agent on the stand. Under oath, he denied he'd said that. If my friend had followed my advice, she could have shown the judge written documentation and would have had a stronger argument—and perhaps could even have filed a claim against the insurance agent.

out and that you have proof of insurance. I also spend about $700 a year to have my own workers' compensation insurance. I don't have any employees, but if one of my contractors is deemed to be my employee because I lost a court case, my own workmans' comp will kick in. I'm not suggesting everyone get it, but talk to your insurance agent about whether you need it.

Segregate Your Assets

If everything you own is in your name and you are sued, you could lose it all. You can use corporations or partnerships to segregate all your activities into different buckets of risk. Let's say you have three businesses. You do real estate investment, which is one bucket. You wholesale houses, another bucket. Maybe you run a construction business or property management company that is high risk. You certainly want to put that in a separate entity—your third bucket. If something happens to one of those entities, you lose only what's in that particular bucket. Right now, if the only bucket you are using is your personal one, you could lose everything.

A wealthy plastic surgeon who was married owned a high-risk business. If something went wrong, he could be sued, so he segregated his assets, putting some of them in his wife's name. For example, he put the vacation home and a large bank account in her name. If he were to be sued, he might lose his practice and some money, but they could still keep the house and bank account—whatever was in his wife's name.

You can do that, too. But watch out: The surgeon's wife ended up marrying the pool boy, and now they own that house and bank account! Be careful about putting assets in family members' names. If you decide to split ownership—some to your spouse, some to your kids—make sure that you trust them completely. There is a better way: Use trusts and corporations; that way you can control your assets and protect them at the same time.

Get Things Out of Your Name

One of my favorite things to do is check out property tax rolls and look up the music and movie stars' homes and see what they paid for them. If the homes are in their names, you can find out when they were bought, for how much, and what the debts are.

Make Deals for Your Kids

Do your kids a favor and make some real estate deals for them. You may want to open a self-directed IRA for each of them so they can earn tax-free income. Buy a house or duplex at a discount and put it in their names or lease-option it. When they're 18 or 20, they'll have a house paid for. I know college will be superexpensive when my son Alexander is ready—by then it will probably be $100,000 a semester or something, so I've taken a few duplexes and put them in his name. By the time he's 18, he'll have property that's paid for. If he's an absolute bum, at least he'll have a duplex to live in and can rent the other side out for beer money. If he wants to go to school, we can sell the duplex and use it to pay for college.

Isn't it interesting that most people will do more for somebody else than they will for themselves? You might find it hard to go out there and do a deal for yourself to make money, but when you're doing something for your loved ones, you'll work five times harder. Maybe the first deal you do shouldn't be for you; maybe you should do it for your spouse or child.

Do you like lawyers having access to that kind of information about you? That's the first thing good lawyers will check if they want to sue you. They want to know if they can collect any money. If you have a big lawsuit against you and you don't own anything and don't have insurance, they're probably not going to get much and thus may not come after you.

If you have mutual funds and bank accounts in your name, you could lose them in a lawsuit. What I do is wrap my investments in an insurance contract, in a life insurance variable annuity based on mutual funds. If I'm sued, they can't get to these assets, because it's almost impossible to attach any type of life insurance contract. To safeguard your money, you may want to sock it away in life insurance.

To take your home out of the public domain, transfer it into a land trust or an irrevocable trust. I don't understand why people who set up living trusts or irrevocable trusts use their own names (e.g., the Anderson Family Living Trust). If you're doing it for anonymity, why use your name? All of my trusts are titled after the property address (e.g., the 1010 Jones Street Trust for the house on 1010 Jones Street). If someone does a title search and look up "Robert Shemin," that house doesn't show up. My advice is to get a land trust and transfer your house into it. This gives you anonymity and some protection.

When you start making money, set up an LLC for each bucket of activities. If you own some rental properties, put those in an LLC. Maybe you're doing a lot of wholesaling—have an LLC that does that, and you can still write off everything. Most attorneys and accountants recommend setting up a limited liability company if you own real estate.

Form a Corporation

There are many types of entities to choose from to take assets out of your name: partnerships, S corporations, C corporations, and limited liability companies. If you line up 100 attorneys and accountants who know real estate, 99 will say that a limited liability company (LLC) is probably the best way to go if you own real estate. It has all the attributes of the others and a lot of flexibility.

Almost anything you do with any other type of corporation or partnership you can do with an LLC. On the other hand, a limited partnership has disadvantages: A general partner would be liable for everything you do (and vice versa), a limited partner cannot participate as a manager. With a limited liability company everyone is protected, there is no general liability, and anyone can be part of management.

Let's say you own 20 houses worth $10 million and they're in your name when you get sued. The court attaches the houses; you can't sell them and you can't refinance them. Your bank account is in your name; the court attaches your bank account and you can't write any checks. Then the court orders the houses to be sold to pay off the judgment.

I like to find successful people and copy them. For example, Marriott Hotels, Hyatt Hotels, and many large apartments are not owned using land trusts; they're owned using limited liability companies. If it's good enough for them to protect a $19 million building, it's good enough for me with my $50,000 or $100,000 duplex.

Say you have 20 houses in a limited liability company and you are the member-manager of the LLC. One of the houses burns down. You're sued for $10 million and lose the judgment. The plaintiffs generally get only a charging order, but they can't break up the company and they can't make you sell your assets. You can still buy and sell houses and refinance them. A charging order states something like this: "We have got a $1 million judgment; you own 80 percent of the stock, so if any money is distributed to you, we get part of it." If your company doesn't distribute any money that year, the plaintiffs won't get it. And they might have to pay taxes on whatever they do get if your LLC is structured properly. Let's say your LLC made $1 million, you owned 80 percent, and the plaintiffs got a charging order for 80 percent of whatever you make. That would be $800,000. But as the managing director of the LLC, you decide that you're not distributing any income this year. They'd have to pay taxes on that $800,000; the IRS doesn't care whether they actually received it or not. The second year that happens, your creditors might want to negotiate with you.

A wealthy man in Arkansas, 78 years old, fell in love with a 23-year-old bartender. His net worth was well over $100 million—but I'm sure it was true love. Before they were married, his lawyer pleaded and begged him to put his assets in limited liability companies and he did.

Surprise, surprise—after about a year of marriage, the young wife divorced her millionaire husband. In a lot of states, when you get divorced, you and your spouse each get half of all the property and assets and income. In this case, if everything had been in his name, she probably would have received 50 percent of it at the time of the divorce. However, his attorney told her attorneys that everything was in limited liability companies. To access it, she could get a charging order and would probably be awarded 50 percent of whatever is distributed from the LLC that year. Even though the LLC earned $10 million that year, if the manager decided not to distribute anything, she would owe taxes on about $5 million with nothing to show for it. The following year, she would have to pay taxes on another $5 million—even if they were not distributing that year, either. Because of this, the lawyers were able to negotiate a more favorable settlement than if everything had been in his name.

Which is the best state to incorporate in? It used to be Delaware. Then it was Nevada. Now it's probably Wyoming. I don't think you have to live there, but you have to have someone in state to represent you. Most lawyers will do that. Certain states try to compete with other states to be the most favorable in which to incorporate. Please check with your own attorney to decide which is the best state for you to incorporate in. Call 866-RSHEMIN, or work with a top-ranked Pre-Paid Legal attorney in your area to answer your questions and help you. Go to www.pre-paidlegal.com/info/shemin.

If your business is passive (i.e., you own real estate but don't manage it yourself), you may not have to register your LLC in your home state. If you're actively involved in a business, which most people are (flipping homes, buying and selling them), then even if you're headquartered in Nevada or Wyoming, you probably still have to register with the state in which you're doing business. You will lose some anonymity, but if someone's really coming after you, they'll uncover everything you own. For a fee, top private investigators in the United States will do a nationwide and international search for your assets. With a few phone calls, they'll locate every corporation you ever owned and possibly every trust in which you had an interest. However, if you and your attorney set things up properly, you will most likely be protected.

Trusts

Land trusts are good, but they can be broken. Generally, in a land trust or *irrevocable trust,* you control everything, and you and your family are the beneficiaries. In a court of law, a good lawyer is going to say you have too much control and that this land trust is a joke. The top asset-protection attorneys I know say land trusts may work in theory, but in court they might not hold up. However, land trusts do offer some anonymity, which is good.

Here's an illustration of this. A person in Atlanta owned 14 properties, all in land trusts. He had a humongous lawsuit against him. The plaintiff's lawyer, who was not a good one, asked if he owned any property. He said no. The lawyer asked if he received income directly from any properties that he owned. He said no and left, because his property was owned in land trusts. He didn't own it; the land trusts did. If the lawyer had asked the question properly—"Have you owned, or do you have any *interest in* any property or entity that owns any property," then he would have had to say yes.

Robert's Tip

If you have an **LLC** or trust that owns property, make sure you and the trust are the named insured, because as soon as you put your property in a land trust, the land trust owns it. If the house burns down and the insurance is in your name, the insurance company may say you don't hold the property any more, so it doesn't have to pay a claim. If you put it into a land trust or corporation, make sure you and the entity are the named insureds. This tip could save you a lot of money.

My friend Scott, an attorney, had a case against a developer in Washington, D.C. He flew there to investigate, and he did a title search on the developer to find out if he owned any property. He couldn't find any because the developer kept all of his property in a land trust and the documents were hidden. Scott said to the judge, "We've got a big lawsuit, he's hiding his assets, and I think he has a trust." The judge issued a court order to the developer to tell Scott what he owned, would own, and was beneficiary to, plus all of his trusts and corporations. Within 24 hours of the court order, the developer had to lay it out on the table or risk being sent to prison. Be warned, if people are serious about coming after you, they can find out what you own. However, if your assets are in a property trust or a corporation, you will probably be protected.

What is a real trust? One in which you don't control the trustee. The trustee is a lawyer, an accountant, a bank. You can't change a real trust. It's not revocable; it's irrevocable. Real trusts cannot be broken in the law. Many wealthy families use irrevocable trusts. They don't control the trustee. Once they're set up, they can't be broken.

Robert's Tips

I recommend looking into getting an irrevocable trust. Get your life insurance out of your estate and out of your name, then put it into an irrevocable life insurance trust so you won't have to pay estate tax when your estate hits the $2 million mark. Usually, your life insurance is in your name and is included in your estate, but if you put $1 million into an irrevocable trust, it's out of your name and therefore out of your estate.

Lease, Don't Own

If you own assets free and clear, people might sue you for them. Instead, set up your corporation to own these assets and you could lease them from your corporation. That protects you from losing assets in a lawsuit.

Use Debt as a Tool

If a house is worth $1 million, and you have $950,000 debt on it, no one will want to collect on that house. But if you own a property free and clear, it's attractive for collectors. Therefore, debt can offer some asset protection. I'm not telling you to accumulate a lot of debt, but a high debt level does make going after your assets less attractive.

Offshore Banking Is No Longer an Option

Before September 11, 2001, banking offshore was the ultimate asset protection technique. A lot of people I know were making high interest rates on their offshore money. They had bank accounts overseas, which they were supposed to declare to the U.S. government, but a lot of people didn't because they took a chance the federal government would never find these accounts.

Since September 11, though, it's very difficult for an American to open an offshore bank account. Unless you're living or doing business offshore, that source of asset protection, once so popular, is finished. Since September 11, our Justice Department and Treasury Department have warned almost every Latin and South American offshore haven not to open bank accounts with Americans, and these banks are falling in line.

Get a 401(k)

If you are sued, it's almost impossible to lose your 401(k) assets. O.J. Simpson had a $30 million civil lawsuit judgment against him. He had to auction off his house, his Heisman trophy, and his personal property. Yet he's still flying around the country golfing and living well in Miami. He's able to do that because of his retirement accounts.

If there are big judgments against you and you lose everything, you can probably keep all of your retirement accounts. Therefore, put a lot of money in pension plans, 401(k)s, self-employment plans, IRAs, and so on.

CHAPTER 13

How you spend your time is more important than how you spend your money.
Money mistakes can be corrected, but time is gone forever.
—DAVID B. NORRIS

Action Plans

To acquire more property without using your own capital, you must focus on your only asset—time. How are you using it?

Focus Your Time

I am an attorney. I don't practice anymore, but I did learn one important lesson from my attorney friends. When you work at many law firms, you have to track your time in 15-minute increments. In fact, a lot of attorneys track their time in six-second increments when talking on the phone, because time is the only thing lawyers have to bill.

Though you may not be an attorney, start tracking your time. It will help your real estate business. Track it every day in 15- or 20-minute increments so you know where your time goes. "Spent 20 minutes talking to the person next to me. Spent 20 minutes thinking about making a phone call. Spent 15 minutes dialing the number. Spent 10 more minutes talking to the person. Spent 20 minutes surfing the Internet. Spent 20 more minutes thinking about where you were going to lunch. Spent 40 minutes going to lunch, and so on." How are you spending your time?

In 1930, a study was done on time management in the United States. Researchers interviewed 1,000 of the most professional, efficient, effective salespeople. Remember, this was in 1930, before all the modern sales training and motivational practices existed. The study found that those salespeople actually worked only about 11 focused hours a week.

A similar study was done in 1998, with researchers studying 1,000 of the most successful, focused, efficient salespeople. After all the training, all the developments in human psychology, all the great motivating people, and all the books and videos, the average salesperson still works only about 11 hours a week!

How many hours are you really working? Six months from now, how many hours would you really work at real estate? How many hours did you spend looking at deals? Track all your hours. Write down what type of property you'd like to wholesale. Develop your focus. Where do you feel comfortable starting? We've already delineated how you're going to find motivated sellers. How much time do you have to spend to find and flip some properties? Would you say 5 hours, 10 hours, 20 hours a week? After you flip a couple and make a profit, you'll want to do it so much, you'll spend all your time flipping.

The next question is, how long do you think it will take to find one decent deal that you might be able to wholesale—30 days, 45 days, 60 days? If you only have 30 minutes to work a week, it will take you much longer. I don't think you can do any business without at least committing five to eight hours a week. That's all. Five to eight *focused* hours a week; most of us have to work 40 hours because we're not focused. I once gave myself 30 days to flip something. I challenge you to wholesale one deal in the next 30 to 60 days. Can you do it? Will you do it? Will you be focused?

If you find the deal, it won't take you long to find the buyer. You're going to the real estate associations; you're talking to Realtors; you're responding to ads in the paper; you might even be running some ads. You are doing what it takes to find these potential buyers. If I find a deal in Las Vegas tomorrow, I simply call the "I buy houses" ads. They are buyers. Once you land a deal, send it out to prospective buyers. Finding buyers is usually the easy part, once you have found a real deal.

Locate a good title company to help you close. How do you find a good title company that knows how to close your wholesale and lease-option deals and that can work with investors? Ask investors. Go to your local real estate association.

When you get going, how many deals would you like to wholesale every month? One? One every quarter? One every six months? Two a month?

After you do your first deal, it becomes easier and easier. I started whole-saling condos in South Beach, Florida. They sell for anywhere from $300,000 to $800,000 and sometimes more. The average profit on one of those ranges from $20,000 to more than $100,000. What kind of prop-erty are you going to do? What area? Write that down and set a goal.

My goal is to do one or two small flips a month in Tennessee, where houses range in price from $50,000 to $150,000. In South Beach, Florida, I try to do one bigger deal, anywhere from $300,000 to $1 mil-lion every quarter. I don't want you just to chase elephants (the super-big deals), spending all of your time working on one big deal. If you can find one bigger apartment building, one shopping center, one chunk of land, one smaller office building up in the hundreds of thousands or several million dollars, you could try to wholesale it. If you find a deal in that range, the buyers are usually easier to deal with because commer-cial buyers have money.

You might start with little deals, then do one bigger deal later. Re-member, when you get into big deals it becomes more competitive. For example, there is not much competition for apartment buildings that consist of 5 to 60 units. Pick a type of property that you like and spe-cialize. Opportunities are everywhere!

Write Down Plans

Take all the notes for your action plans that you started writing and, for the next several minutes, write down the actions and activities you'll do this week, next week, and the following weeks to find deals. Here are some key components of your plan.

Decide how much free time you have to put into real estate investing. You may have only five hours a week because you're busy, or you may want to pursue this full-time.

Decide how you're going to find deals. Run an ad, drive for dollars, go to auctions, go to the real estate association, hand out fliers, call Realtors, and so on.

Now make a one-week plan, a 30-day plan, a 60-day plan, and a 90-day plan. Over the next 90 days, consistently look for deals, set goals, and

Humor Helps!

An investor I was trying to close a deal with just wouldn't return my phone calls. He's busy, like everybody. I called him one day, left a message asking him to call me back, and he didn't. I called the next day. I called him 17 days in a row before he finally returned my phone call. I'm always polite. I never get upset. As a matter of fact, I use humor. After a few days, I said, "Look, obviously you're not calling me back; you might be on a three-week vacation; you might have been abducted by aliens and are unable to return my phone call; maybe you've been kidnapped and are tied up in a basement. Or you might be getting frustrated that I'm calling so much and don't ever want to talk to me. Call me and let me know which reason it is." After that message, he laughed and called me. That's why I recommend always being polite, but persistent. My policy and procedure is to call specific people every day until they call me back. What's your policy?

make offers. When you're looking for deals, write the following on the bottom of your data sheet: "My goal is to make five offers next week. The next week, I'm going to make 10 offers. The week after that, I'm going to make 20 offers."

The most difficult part of finding a good deal is reaching people. How many of you become frustrated when you call people and they don't call back? Understand that if you make 100 calls, you'll likely talk to only 10 or 15 people. Leave a message that *motivates* people to call you back. Be honest. Perhaps you can say that you have cash for them or that you need to buy 10 houses soon, so please call back soon.

No-Money-Down Plans

Write down your favorite one or two ways to buy property with no money down. Maybe you have perfect credit and are going to borrow money. Maybe you don't have any money or credit, and you want to wholesale, lease-option, and find a partner with money. Maybe you really love zero-financing opportunities and making full-price offers, so you focus on that.

Write down your answers to the following:

- How many deals would you like to do in the next 30 days, 60 days, 90 days? _____

- How many calls will you have to make on properties to find those deals? _____

- How much time will you spend doing it? _____

■ How many properties would you like to have at the end of the year? Two years and three years from now? _____ _____ _____

Go to the mortgage company or bank and ask for preapproval so you'll know where you stand. Also, line up one or two partners with money and find a hard moneylender. You're going to need them, because even if you sell a property to other investors, they might need money, so you need to have sources.

If you have zero money invested, your return is infinite.

Dealing with Advice

Don't let other people stop you from buying property without using your own money. Do you have family, relatives, or friends who are trying to dissuade you from getting into real estate because they think you're crazy for even reading this? Let me show you how to fix that. We tend to get advice from three types of people. From this moment forward, anytime people give you advice, put them in one of three categories. This will not only help you in real estate investing, but in your business life, spiritual life, and personal life.

We get most of our advice from people in category one: those who have absolutely no clue what they are talking about. Do the people who are giving you real estate advice deal in real estate? No, but they tell you what doesn't work. Right? We get most of our advice from people who have no clue.

In category two are people who have done something, failed miserably at it, and love to tell you about it. "I bought the real estate course advertised on TV. I made two phone calls. It didn't work for me. It won't work for you." Well, my friend who has been married five times wants to give out relationship advice, too, but I'm not buying it. Those who fail at something love to give out advice.

In category number three are the experts—people who have accomplished something, who are involved in the industry, who have been successful, who have stuck with it. These are the people whose advice you should listen to.

When I was first starting in real estate, one of my close relatives said, "This is crazy. How can you sell something you don't own? That's must be illegal; you are going to get arrested. Don't even tell me about it, or I'll be implicated in it." This relative continued to say, "I don't want to hear about your real estate deals. Don't tell me about them." Other family members also came to me and said, "Please don't include us in any of this real estate business, because if you get in trouble, we don't want to go down with you." They said it wouldn't work. I felt awful because I wasn't getting support.

One day I went to a closing. I had found a little house for $40,000 that was worth $60,000, so I flipped it to someone for $45,000 and netted about $5,000. The day of the closing, I went home with my check and turned it over to that doubting family member. On the back of the check I wrote, "Pay to the order of [her name]" and signed it. I told her to cash it and blow it—buy some clothes, take a trip, do something crazy, just blow it. She asked where I got the check. I said I flipped a house. She asked how I did that. I said I found a motivated seller, put it under contract for $40,000 even though it was worth about $60,000, and found a buyer who paid $45,000. Then she asked, "How many houses did you flip today? When are you doing another one?"

A few days later, she asked, "Have you flipped any more houses?" I said, "No but I've got one coming up." The following week I flipped another one and made about $8,200. She said, "How much did you get it under contract for?" I said $70,000. She asked what it was worth, and I told her $100,000. Then she surprised me by saying, "How come you made only eight? Get out there, boy. Get going. Go, go, go!"

My philosophy is to be silent but deadly. Go out there and flip a few houses, then give a check or cash to the person closest to you who is the most skeptical.

Getting What You Want

Here are some techniques for getting what you want.

Reward Yourself

When you get paid after wholesaling a house or doing a no-money-down deal, take 10 percent of it and do something fun. Reward yourself. As business owners and real estate investors, we work, work, work, make, make, make, and we rarely reward ourselves. Get a massage, take a trip, go on a picnic, jump out of an airplane (with a parachute) . . . do something fun.

Set goals for rewarding yourself. After you wholesale three houses and make $10,000 or $15,000, take $1,000 and go on a cruise. I know, you may have to pay off your debt and pay your bills. Do that, but don't forget to reward yourself.

Build Your Savings

Take 10 percent of the money from each deal and save it. I don't care if you've got Visa banging on your door, the rent payments are falling behind, and everybody is coming after you. Take 10 percent, put it away, invest it in something solid, and don't touch it. Pay yourself first.

Would you be feeling more comfortable now if you'd been doing that for the past 10 years? If you save $89 a week at 11 percent interest, in 30 years you'll have more than $1 million. If you save $89 a week and earn 18 percent, which isn't difficult in real estate, in 30 years you'll have more than $5 million. So start paying yourself first by building your savings.

Robert's Tips

My personal trainer at the gym told me to write down how much I exercised and what I ate every day so we could track the data. I wanted to, but I got busy and didn't do it. He asked me about it every day. I said I'd do it. But I didn't do it. Finally, he said, "Robert, every day you don't bring in your write-up, you have to give me $25." I decided that was an expensive way to blow $25, so I started writing things down.

I suggest you go to a loved one—a spouse, relative, partner, or friend—and say, "Every Friday I need to do this report, and if I don't do it, I'll give you 50 bucks." You have to motivate yourself. It's hard to do.

This has made an unbelievable difference in my life. Most of us spend our money right away, but you'll be a lot better off if you take at least 10 percent of it and sock it away. Also remember that you will have to pay taxes on your profits, so start managing your finances. Record what comes in and what goes out, and review those figures every Friday.

Friday Activity Check-in

Every Friday, look at your activity, what you did and how much money you made. Even if you didn't do any real estate business last week, write down on a sheet of paper whatever you did do and look at it. It will it remind you to do more toward your real estate goals.

What Holds You Back?

What holds most of us back is doubt or fear. When has fear served you? If you're not getting what you want in life, in business, in real estate, if you're not making offers, not getting your business going, not doing what you need to do, not getting the education you want, not earning the money or success you want, what's holding you back? Probably fear and doubt. Beliefs such as, "I can't do this; I'm not good enough; I shouldn't do it."

Another thing that holds people back (and I fall victim to this, too) is pride. Successful people may read through these materials and say, "I'm too smart. I'm too sophisticated. I don't need to do that. I'm not going to do that business. I'm not going to make 100 offers a week. I'm not going to make all those calls responding to rent ads. I'm not going to get involved with this or try that." When has pride served you? It doesn't.

The cure for pride, doubt, and fear is *action*. If you're not getting what you want, take action. Make a phone call. Do some research to find the answer. Shoot out more offers. Get involved in the business. Get more training. Get an education. Go, go, go. Just take action. That's the simple recipe for success.

Brad Didn't Know Fear

Some time ago, I was giving a seminar and asked everyone to stand up and clap. Most people stood up and gave it half of their energy; a few people got into it. At the first table was a guy, Brad, about 21 years old. He got up on the table and started jumping up and down. I started thinking, "Oh my God, we're going to be sued . . . he's going to kill somebody, injure himself, knock down the tables." Brad had no fear or doubt—and he obviously had no pride.

In fact, Brad had no real estate training, no background. He used to wear about 20 earrings, had red-and-purple hair, and answered the phone in some pizza place for about eight bucks an hour. Brad's story is interesting because his family kicked him out of the house. He didn't know what he wanted to do, but he said, "Robert, this real estate seems like it might work. Just tell me what to do and I'll do it." He became very focused and within six weeks wholesaled his first house and made $8,000. The week after that, he did another deal and made $7,000. In his first year—12 months from the time he took that course and jumped up and down on the table—he made over $100,000. I'm proud to say that he's now lease-optioning and controls about $1 million net of real estate. He makes over $100,000 a year. He's set.

Brad is now 24 years old. Why did he succeed where a lot of other people didn't? Because he had no fear or doubt. He took action. Brad goes to raves and makes world music and does vibe stuff and stays up all night. He works only about two to four hours a day some days, but when he does work, he's focused, making a lot of calls and looking at a lot of properties.

Some students ask about going further—can I coach or mentor them? Over the years, I have taken on a couple of private students, and I've been recruiting the right people to help me do this. We work one-on-one with people to take them to the next level. We do weekly coaching and training and we're available for questions, problems, and help needed with deals. We have helped a lot of students get to the next level quickly. We've also found opportunities to do deals together and help people in ways that are really beneficial.

My challenge to you is go out there and get started. When you're having trouble, think of somebody who's really successful. *You can do this.* People with fewer skills than you possess have done it. When you run into a roadblock, think about who you can call to get an answer that will help you move forward. Set your goals. Let me know about your success. I'm available for you; I get a lot of satisfaction out of that.

Your 40-Day Plan for Success

For a free report that includes specific action steps to take every day and every week to accelerate your investments, call 888-302-8018. Ask for "Your 40-Day Plan for Success"—a $50 value that's free just for asking.

Tax Reduction Strategies Pertaining to Foreclosure Transactions

This chapter was written by Albert Aiello, CPA, MA, a licensed real estate broker with more than 25 years of tax experience specializing in real estate and 1031 exchanges. He is an author, national lecturer, and graduate tax professor.

This chapter addresses:

1. Structuring entities when first acquiring foreclosure properties
2. Maximizing tax deductions related to foreclosures
3. Paying little or no taxes when flipping foreclosures
4. Additional tax strategies

Welcome to the Profitable Business of Foreclosures

Many consider foreclosures to be the most lucrative aspect of real estate investing for several reasons:

1. *Less competition—"underground."* The foreclosure marketplace is often tagged as the "underground" of real estate investing as opposed to the usual retail world of real estate. This means less competition from retail or uneducated buyers.

2. *Less competition—specialized knowledge.* While you do not have to be a brain surgeon to be successful in foreclosure investing, you should have above-average acumen to understand the legal aspects of foreclosures in the state (or states) in which you will be doing business. (Each state has its own set of laws pertaining to foreclosures.) Many investors and wanna-bes will be discouraged by the additional complexity in the foreclosure business.

3. *Overpaying and overleveraging in the retail market.* In many parts of the country, real estate has experienced a rapidly escalating market in a relatively short time. In this type of market you have a frenzy of buying, in which anxious and highly emotional retail buyers overpay for properties and, in many cases, also overmortgage them. These types of buyers often find themselves in over their heads with other types of debts as well (e.g., leased automobiles and credit cards). When the economy slows down and companies start to downsize, these homeowners often lose their jobs. Recent substantial stock market losses worsen this recessionary scenario even further. Homeowners find themselves in a financial bind, unable to meet

their obligations, including their mortgage payments. We now have a highly motivated seller.

The combination of less competition and more distressed sellers renders the opportunity for substantial profits in foreclosures for the savvy, educated entrepreneur. Large profits from foreclosure "flippers" and "keepers" translates into potential tax liabilities that can drain your foreclosure gains unless you plan correctly in advance of the transactions. Thus, the purpose of this bonus chapter is to minimize your taxes from profitable foreclosure transactions.

Keep in mind that the tax strategies pertaining to foreclosure transactions are pretty much the same as for nonforeclosure transactions. However, as previously discussed, larger foreclosure profits mean larger and often unexpected tax liabilities that significantly deplete your gains.

Therefore, there is the necessity to implement tax reduction planning with a specialized and focused approach via this chapter, which is a supplement to *The Real Estate Investor's Goldmine of Brilliant Tax Strategies* or the Goldmine. Accordingly, references will be made to the Goldmine.

Strategies When You First Acquire Your Foreclosure Properties: Entity Structuring for the Right Ownership Form

Flips: LLC Partnerships or Limited Partnerships

Many of you will generate quick cash from flipping your foreclosure bargains. As discussed in Goldmine Section 6, if you are just beginning to flip properties, you will follow the appropriate Goldmine strategies in Section 41 and 42 and take the position that you are not a dealer and do not start off as a corporation (with its many disadvantages). Instead, start off as an LLC partnership (or as a limited partnership if your state heavily taxes LLCs) as per Goldmine Section 6. Because you are taking the Goldmine position that you are not a dealer, your flip profits will not be subject to Social Security taxes. With a partnership as a pass-through entity, you can also use rental losses from your keepers to offset the flip profits to reduce income taxes in addition to the Social Security taxes. Also, because you are taking the Goldmine position that you are not a dealer, when you sell you can defer income taxes on the gain via a 1031 exchange (covered later). If you hold any of the financing, you can defer income taxes on the gain via installment sale reporting under Internal Revenue Code Section 453.

Flips: Self-Directed Retirement Plans

If you do not immediately need the cash from your foreclosure flips, then use a self-directed retirement plan to buy and sell your nondealer foreclosure flips, free of *all* taxes. Again, because you are taking the Goldmine position that you are not a dealer, you can defer taxes within a retirement plan. The tax-deferred profits in the plan will compound to a much larger accumulated sum than they would outside the plan. These tax-deferred accumulated sums can be further invested into more flips or other profitable investments. Besides an IRA, you can also have a self-directed SEP, Simple, or Keogh retirement plan, thus doing foreclosure transactions that are highly profitable, but tax-deferred. Plus, with a Roth self-directed IRA, the profits are permanently tax-free!

Tax tip on taking cash out of your IRA: Take out penalty-free and income-tax-free cash from your retirement plans. One of the ways you can receive IRA funds without incurring penalty (even if you are younger than age 59½) is to receive a lifetime annuity schedule of essentially equal payments. (Have a pension specialist do this for you.) There is a way to tap your plan for not only a penalty-free annuity, but also one that is income-tax-free and payment-free. This is done by obtaining a home-equity loan with a loan payment about the same as the IRA annuity. Here, you will have two very positive offsets:

1. A cash offset, where your loan payment going out is offset by your IRA annuity coming in.
2. A tax offset, where the deductible interest from your home-equity loan payment offsets your taxable IRA annuity payment.

Example

After determining the amount of annuity payments you can receive, you take out a home equity loan at the same amount of payments. Assume you can take out $500 a month as an IRA annuity and that $500 a month will enable you to obtain a home-equity loan of $50,000. The $500 incoming IRA annuity offsets your $500 outgoing loan payment, while the loan interest offsets your taxable IRA annuity.

Result

You'll have a $50,000 lump sum of penalty-free, tax-free, and payment-free cash, which you can invest to earn more income!

Assume you invest the $50,000 in real estate at an annual yield of 20 percent a year. You'll have $10,000 a year annual income that is totally sheltered by property deductions, via the Goldmine, and is therefore tax-free!

Result

You used your IRA annuity in a tax-favored manner to generate another $10,000 tax-free income every year . . . plus the equity buildup in the property.

Money makes money, but tax-free money makes a whole lot more money!

Tax tip

Another way to take out penalty-free and tax-free cash from your retirement plans is to borrow from your Keogh plan. As of January 1, 2002, single proprietors and partners can borrow from their Keogh plans, and S corporation shareholders can borrow from their plans. The loan cannot exceed one-half of the vested interest in the plan up to $50,000. However, this is tax-free money to you, plus you deduct the interest on the loan, and the plan does not have to report it (double taxation the right way—your way!).

Example

You borrow $25,000 from your Keogh plan and must pay the plan 8 percent interest for five years. The $25,000 is tax-free money to you, plus you deduct the interest on the loan, and the plan does not have to report it. You invest the $25,000 in real estate for an annual yield of 20 percent a year, or $5,000 a year income from the tax-free borrowed money.

Alert

While you can borrow from Keogh plans, you cannot borrow from SEP, Simple, and IRA plans. You also cannot use any of these plans (including Keogh's) as security for a loan. If you do borrow from these plans

(SEP, Simple, and IRA) or use any of them as security for a loan, there can be substantial taxes and penalties.

Tip

If you do not have earned income eligible for retirement plan contributions, form a separate management company for your keepers. From your keeper property income, you pay the management company fees for various services the company performs. These fees are earned income and thus eligible for retirement plan contributions. See Goldmine Section 7-A.

Tip with Sheriff's Sales

To acquire foreclosures at sheriff's sales within your self-directed plan, you must draw the money in advance from the retirement plan account with the bank check payable to the sheriff (or whomever, just *not* you). Here, you may have to estimate. It is better to be over. Any excess could be directly returned to the plan account.

Full-Time Dealer-Flippers

For entity structuring for full-time dealer-flippers, refer to Goldmine Section 6-A.

Keepers: LLC Partnerships or Limited Partnerships

If you want to keep and rent out your foreclosure bargains, then generally the ideal ownership entity is an LLC partnership. If your state heavily taxes LLC profits, then you may need to use a limited partnership. Refer to Goldmine Section 5-A for a further discussion.

Keepers: Self-Directed Plans for Large Cash Flow Keepers with Taxable Income

Generally you do not want to buy keepers in a self-directed retirement plan. However, if you follow the techniques of buying foreclosures from the experts (such as Ernie Kessler or Dwan & Sharon), you will be buying your properties at deep discounts. This will include properties that you intend to keep and rent out. If you buy these discounted bargains for cash and own them free and clear, then these properties can generate substantial cash flow even after tax deductions for depreciation, taxes, and operating expenses.

Example

You acquire a bargain property for all cash. Taxes, insurance, and other operating expenses are $3,000 a year. You obtain a tenant for $700 a month, or $8,400 a year, leaving you with a positive cash flow of $5,400. Tax depreciation is $1,000 a year. Your after-taxable net income on the property is $4,400 ($5,400 less depreciation of $1,000). In a 31 percent tax bracket, you would have to pay $1,360 in taxes on the $4,400. In a rounded 40 percent tax bracket, you would have to pay $1,760 in taxes on the $4,400. If you owned 10 of these properties (many investors own much more), you would have to pay 10 times the amount in taxes—$13,600 or $17,600, respectively.

You can avoid all of these taxes by acquiring these properties within a self-directed plan.

Also, you pay *no* taxes on the profits! Keep in mind that if your self-directed plan sells any of these properties, the profit, regardless of size, is not taxed. Remember, while there is a limit on the amount of annual retirement plan contributions, there is *no* limit on the amount that a retirement plan can earn, tax-free.

Tax Tip

You may not want to acquire these types of properties within your retirement plan if you have other deductions to offset the property's taxable income.

Alert on Using Financing

All retirement plan mortgage loans must be nonrecourse: Any loans on property that you acquire within your plan must be nonrecourse. A *nonrecourse mortgage* is one for which the debtor is not personally liable on the debt. With a nonrecourse mortgage, you and your plan trustee are not personally liable. In the event of default, the lender takes only the property, not the other assets of the buyer-borrower. (Note: Many hard moneylenders give nonrecourse loans.)

It is the author's opinion that little or no debt should be used to buy real estate within your retirement plan for these reasons:

1. The interest is not deductible against your income outside of the plan.
2. Any debt (even nonrecourse) could increase risk. For the most part, free-and-clear properties should be the preferred retirement plans where safety is especially important.
3. The loan must be nonrecourse as just explained. While this is favorable to you and your retirement plan, it could involve more hassles to find these types of loans.

Maximizing Deductions While You Own Your Foreclosure Acquisitions: Short- and Long-Term Acquisitions

Deductions for Short-term Foreclosure Acquisitions (Flips)

Regarding claim depreciation, even if you will be quickly selling your foreclosure bargain acquisitions in the same year, you should still take depreciation deductions for any property that you have taken title to. This will help avoid dealer status per Goldmine Section 42 (Strategy 10).

Important Tax Pointer

Even if the bargain flip was bought and sold in your self-directed retirement plan, you will want to claim depreciation for the same reason previously stated—to help avoid dealer status per Goldmine Section 42 (Strategy 10).

Claim all deductions if you will be buying your foreclosure bargain in one year and selling the following year. You take deductions (depreciation, repairs, etc.) in the earlier year, but don't pay taxes until the following year when you sell the property. Upon the sale, you will have to recapture certain deductions (e.g., depreciation and repairs), but you have the immediate use of the tax savings in the earlier year. When you sell the property the following year, you will not have to pay the deferred taxes until the following April, or a year and three months later (barring any requirements for quarterly estimated taxes). In the meantime, you can invest the tax savings into more real estate and for additional income.

Additional Tax Savers

This strategy will save you even more taxes if any of the following happen:

- You are in a lower bracket in the later year of sale.

- You pay lower capital gains taxes in the later year of sale if you hold the property for more than a year. (See Goldmine Section 9 for a further discussion.)

- You defer the taxes in the later year of sale via a 1031 exchange or installment sale (IRC 453) because you avoid dealer status as per Goldmine Section 42.

Deduction Strategies

Given the preceding, claim the following deductions in the earlier year:

- Write off the old components being replaced during any rehabbing as per IRS Regulation 1.167(a)-8. (See Section 14 of the Goldmine for a further discussion.)

Example

An entrepreneur, E, buys a property for $80,000, and it's worth $130,000. E does a breakdown of all property components. E completely guts and replaces a number of these components. These old components are being retired and are nonfunctioning. They are listed here along with their original allocated cost:

Bathroom	$4,044
Flooring	2,327
Heating	3,860
Plumbing	4,150
Roof	3,061
Walls, internal	10,638
Kitchen	6,700
Total	$34,780

The $34,780 of retired components can be fully written off all in one year as an ordinary deduction without passive loss or alternative minimum tax limits. In a 31 percent tax bracket, that's an immediate tax savings of more than $10,780!

• Claim depreciation deductions as previously discussed and as per Goldmine Section 12-A. See also Goldmine Section 15 on claiming deprecation deductions on vacant property.

Tax Reminder

This strategy is also to avoid dealer status per Goldmine Section 42.

• Write off repairs. As much as possible, segment any rehabbing costs as fully deductible repairs. See Goldmine Sections 17 to 19-A (including the case study on converting capital improvements into deductible repairs in Section 19-A).

• Deduct interest on any loans as per Goldmine Section 22.

• Claim other deductions as per Goldmine Section 23.

The following example illustrates the favorable cash impact of claiming these deductions for flips, even though the property is sold the following year.

Example

Favorable cash impact: Rhonda Rehab incurs $50,000 in deductions in the first year of rehabbing her house. Assuming a rounded tax bracket of 30 percent, Rhonda pockets $15,000 in tax savings. She then sells the property the next year at a gain. It is true that the taxes are only deferred, not eliminated. However, Rhonda does not have to pay the deferred taxes until the following April, or a year and three months later (barring any requirements for quarterly estimated taxes). In the meantime, she has effectively employed the time value of money by having the tax dollars now to invest for additional earnings. If the $15,000 deferred tax savings generated a 10 percent yield in a year and three months, the earnings would be almost $2,000. At 15 percent, the earnings would be more than $3,000. Suppose Rhonda used the $15,000 to buy a bargain property and quickly flipped it for a clear profit of $20,000. Now she can take that $20,000 and make, say, $15,000. Then she can take that $15,000 and make another $15,000 and so on. There are many more income opportunities when the cash is in *your* hands, not the IRS's.

Deductions for Longer-Term Foreclosure Acquisitions

These will be many for rental keepers.

1. Depreciate with full componentizing as per Goldmine Sections 12 to 16-A.

2. Write off the old components being replaced during any rehabbing of your rentals as per IRS Regulation 1.167(a)-8. (See Section 14 of the Goldmine for further discussion.)

3. Write off repairs of your rentals per Goldmine Sections 17 to 19-A.

4. Deduct interest on any loans on your rentals as per Goldmine Section 22.

5. Claim other Goldmine deductions as per Goldmine Section 23.

6. Claim more deductions pertinent to the foreclosure and distressed property business:

   ▪ Auto expenses to check out distressed properties, visit preforeclosure homeowners and banks

   ▪ Ads in newspapers and other publications—"I buy houses" ads

- Ads in newspapers and other publications to sell your foreclosure properties
- Appraisal fees—foreclosures and other properties
- Assumption fees for taking over mortgages of preforeclosures and other properties
- Attaché case for foreclosure forms and other real estate forms
- Accountant's fees pertaining to foreclosures and other accounting matters in your business
- Attorney's fees pertaining to foreclosures and other legal matters in your business
- Batteries for flashlights, cameras, and other business paraphernalia
- Books, tapes, publications, software on foreclosures
- Books, tapes, publications, software on related real estate topics
- Brochures about your real estate investment company, specializing in foreclosures
- Business cards and other stationery that you use as a foreclosure investor—"I buy houses"
- Business plan for your foreclosure business (books, tapes, software, etc.)
- Calculators (financial) to do the foreclosure math and other real estate computations
- Camera (digital) for taking pictures of distressed houses (and sending to the lender)
- Cleaning supplies to clean out trashed foreclosed and distressed properties

- Computer for your foreclosure business

- Computer supplies and accessories for your foreclosure business

- Credit cards—dues and interest if credit card used solely for your foreclosure and real estate business

- Database software for buyers, sellers, banks, attorneys, investors, and so on

- Dictionary of banking terms (*Barron's business guides*) so you can speak bankers' language

- Directories, including crisscross or phone directories (that you pay for) to locate distressed sellers

- Directories of attorneys, especially foreclosure and real estate attorneys

- Directories of accountants, especially foreclosure and real estate accountants

- Entertainment (lunch, dinner, etc.) for leads on bargain foreclosure buys

- Eviction costs and other fees related to removing former homeowner of foreclosed property

- Exhibit equipment and supplies to display your business at seminars and conventions

- Fees to title companies or courthouse employees for searches on foreclosure properties

- Fees to bird dogs for finding information on bargain properties

- Other fees related to your foreclosure and real estate business

- Flowers to homeowners and to those who find information on bargain properties

- "I buy houses" flyers to distribute all over the place
- Flyers to sell your foreclosure properties
- Gifts (limited to $25) to finders of information on bargain properties
- Greeting cards (with your company name) to homeowners and finders of information
- Hardware and supplies for quick repairs to your foreclosed properties
- Internet expenses and advertising for your foreclosure business
- Laptop (notebook) computer to take with you for negotiations with homeowner or on travel
- Dictionary of legal terms, including foreclosure terminology
- Legal forms (agreements, contracts, leases, etc.)
- Locks, keys, and quicksets to change locks on your foreclosed properties
- Lockbox for easy showing of your foreclosure properties for sale
- Mailing costs to homeowners in preforeclosure—postage, stationery, handling
- Mailing costs to banks for REOs and short sales—postage, stationery, handling
- Mailing costs to attract cash investors to help finance foreclosure buys
- Mailing lists of homeowners in foreclosures and distressed sellers
- Mailing lists of investors as a source of cash for your bargain buys
- Maps and atlases to locate distressed properties

- Marketing costs to promote your foreclosure business
- Mortgage amortization—book, calculator, or software
- Multiple listing service (MLS) fees to find distressed properties and motivated sellers
- Measuring tools and devices to check out distressed properties
- Newspapers, legal, foreclosure listings (purchase or subscription)
- Newspapers, other, listing properties for sale and legal notices (purchase or subscription)
- Notary fees for legal documents
- Notary licenses, bonding and renewals (for legal documents)
- Notepads and clipboard to evaluate distressed properties
- Odor-Xit to kill the foulest of odors in distressed properties (1-877-ODORXIT, Dept. 101)
- Phone and/or cell phone for your foreclosure business
- Photographs of distressed houses (and sending to the lender)
- Photo supplies and accessories
- Pre-Paid Legal Services pertaining to foreclosures and other legal matters in your business
- Prepayment penalty for early payoff of a mortgage
- Publications on foreclosure lists and courthouse information
- Real estate data, such as REDI (cost or subscription)
- Record-keeping software such as Quicken or Quick Books for your foreclosure business
- Recording (and other) fees for legal documents

- Seminars (cost of) on foreclosures to attract distressed sellers, motivated buyers, and investors
- Shirts, jackets, or other apparel with "I buy houses" information
- Signs on your lawn or some prominent location ("I buy houses")
- Signs on your car ("I buy houses")
- Signs (sales) to sell your foreclosure properties
- Tape recorder (to record courthouse records and other business matters)
- Tools for repairs to foreclosure properties
- Toys or games (safe ones) for homeowner's children to play with during foreclosure negotiations
- Thank you cards to referral sources of foreclosures
- Out-of-town travel expenses to check out properties and to visit preforeclosure homeowners and banks
- TV used solely for business-related video and Internet
- Video equipment and VCRs to view foreclosures and other distressed properties

Note: Not only are these deductions often overlooked, but they can also serve as reminders of what you should do and what you need in your foreclosure business. That includes engaging Pre-Paid Legal Services for ongoing expert legal advice at a very low cost, placing a sign on your car, and using lockboxes, business cards, legal newspapers, directories, digital cameras, and so on.

How to Pay Few or No Taxes When You Flip or Sell Your Foreclosure Properties

Strategies

First, avoid being a dealer per Goldmine Section 42. By avoiding being a dealer, you can now employ strategies 2 to 5.

Second, buy and sell in your self-directed retirement plan as previously discussed in this report.

Tax Pointer

In order to use a self-directed retirement plan to defer taxes on profits, the property must have been originally acquired by the plan and not by you.

Tax Tip

If you did not originally buy the property in a self-directed retirement plan, then sell the property you own outside of your plan to an unrelated (but friendly) party in an arm's-length transaction. Subsequent to this, your plan buys the property from this unrelated party. Now the property is in your self-directed retirement plan (and all property income can now be tax-deferred). As much as possible, the two transactions should be documented as separate transactions. Timewise, do the transactions as far as apart as possible, preferably in different tax years. This should be technically okay, but is not an absolute guarantee. Seek able advice.

Defer taxes on the sale via a 1031 exchange:

- For your keepers, 1031 exchanges are Ideal for saving a bundle of taxes. See Goldmine Sections 32 to 34-A.
- For your flippers, see "Flipping Properties and 1031 Exchanges" next.

- For acquiring replacement properties at a sheriff's sale in a 1031 exchange, see the end of this section, "Foreclosure Replacement Properties in a 1031 Exchange."

If you take back paper, defer taxes via installment sale reporting (IRC 453). See Goldmine Sections 35 and 37.

Hold the property for more than a year and incur lower-taxed capital gains. See Goldmine Section 9.

Look for tax losses or deductions to reduce taxable gain, especially from the rental losses of your keepers. (This is one of several reasons why those who flip properties should also have long-term keepers.) Also, look for other tax losses or deductions to reduce taxable gain. For example, any loser stocks or bonds that can be sold by the end of the year will generate capital losses that can be used to fully offset any capital gains from real estate. A business loss, retirement plan contribution, and many other deductions can do the same. Loss strategies are further discussed in Goldmine Sections 27 and 44.

Use other tax-reduction strategies for sales from Goldmine Section 31.

The overall favorable impact is that you have the best of two worlds: up-front deductions for immediate tax savings, yet few or no taxes on the sale.

By using the preceding tax reduction sale strategies, you can reap high deductions in one year, yet pay little or no taxes in the year of sale. For instance, you can use the deductions to reduce ordinary income with rates as high as 40 percent, yet when you sell the property, you pay zero taxes via the powerful 1031 exchange.

Flipping Properties and 1031 Exchanges

Holding Requirement
The 1031 exchanges are subject to a number of IRS requirements. One of these is that both the relinquished and the replacement property must be *held* (emphasis added) for investment or business use, according to Internal Revenue Code Section 1031(a)(1). This requirement is known as the *holding requirement*.

IRS Interpretation
The IRS interprets this holding requirement to mean that both the relinquished and the replacement property must be held for a certain time period.

Holding Requirement in Relation to Quick Flips
Accordingly, conventional thinking is that a quick flip of a property will not qualify for the tax deferral benefits of a 1031 exchange because of this exchange holding requirement.

No Specific Time Period
But there is no specific, objective holding (time) period requirement for both the relinquished and the replacement property.

IRS Viewpoint on Time Period
In an IRS letter ruling, the IRS ruled that a two-year holding period would be sufficient to meet this holding period test (IRS Letter Ruling 8429039). In 1989, there was an IRS proposal (never enacted) of one year.

Tax Courts Take More Liberal Viewpoint on Time Period
However, IRS letter rulings, and certainly proposals, do not have the force or effect of law.

Accordingly, the tax courts have been much more lenient in ascertaining that a property has been held long enough to qualify for Section 1031 tax-free treatment. In one case, nine months was deemed sufficient [Wagenson 74 TC 683 1980]. In another case, six months was enough [124 Front St. Inc. 65 TC 6 (1975), 1976-2CB 3]. In Allegheny County Auto Mart, Inc., the property was held five days before the sale/exchange [TC Memo (1953)]. In Rutherford, the transfer was immediate [TC Memo 1978-505]. See also Bolker, 81 TC 782 (1983) and Mageneson, 81 TC 767 (1983). Bolker and Mageneson involved the immediate changes of ownership. According to the courts, such changes did not violate the exchange. However, the IRS's position is that they do violate the exchange [IRS Rev. Rulings 75-292 & 77-337].

Time Period: IRS Versus Tax Courts

Based on the preceding, the IRS's position would appear to favor a holding (time) period of one to two years, whereas the tax court's position is anywhere from immediate to nine months.

The Conclusion with Flips

Quick flips will probably not qualify within the IRS, but may qualify in the eyes of the tax court. Accordingly, doing a 1031 exchange for a flip is generally going to be riskier, with wholesaling (as opposed to retailing) being the riskiest of all, especially the assignment of contracts. However, it will not be illegal because there is no safe-harbor time period, and you have a defensible position with the aforementioned tax court decisions.

Tax Tip

Consider extending the holding period with a short to midterm lease/option. This would help to ensure favorable 1031 tax-free recognition. Here, you help to avoid dealer status on the flips by demonstrating that you have also have "rental/investment" intent with your property, as per the Supreme Court case William Malat, discussed in Goldmine Section 41 and Appendix E.

1031 Tax Tip

Engage a qualified intermediary (QI) that specializes in complex exchanges, such as those combined with flips. One such QI is National Exchange Services, Inc. (NESI), which has done exchanges in more than 40 states. (Call 1-800-351-1031.)

Overall Planning Tip

For those who want to use 1031 exchanges for flips, follow the planning strategies to avoid the "dealer taint," discussed in Section 42 of *The Real Estate Investor's Goldmine of Tax Strategies*. You especially want to adhere to the strategies in Goldmine Section 42-A for avoiding dealer status by reducing your chances of an IRS audit. Reason: *No* audit = *no* controversy = *no* problem!

Foreclosure Replacement Properties in a 1031 Exchange

In a number of exchanges for replacement property, prudent investors snap up excellent buys (often called "steals") through foreclosures. With preforecloses or REOs, there is usually no problem with the mechanics of the exchange. They generally occur as any other normal 1031 transaction. However, there can be more difficulty at the sheriff's sale. Some of the potential problems follow:

45-day Identification Requirements.

One of the essential requirements of a 1031 exchange is that replacement properties be identified within a time period that is no later than midnight of the forty-fifth day following the settlement of the relinquished property. The 45 ID letter must clearly designate the specific legal descriptions of the properties. Generally, with a foreclosure sale, investors don't know exactly which property they want or whether they will successfully bid on the property. Of course, it is possible that they do know and they could make the proper and timely written identification.

1031 Tax Tip

An exception to the 45 ID requirement is that any replacement property closed on within the 45 days is deemed to be automatically identified. No written ID is necessary. It would be much better for the investor to buy the foreclosed property within the 45-day time frame. With foreclosure types of sales, such quick closings are not only possible, but also frequently probable. See Goldmine Section 33 for 45 ID rules.

Alert

Try to avoid buying foreclosures (especially at sheriff's sales) before the settlement of the relinquished property. Otherwise, if you must buy the replacement property first, you would have to do a reverse "Starker" exchange. For more about reverse exchanges, see section VIII-13 of *The 1031 Money Machine,* or contact a 1031 exchange specialist (1-800-351-1031).

Deposits

In a standard 1031 transaction, earnest money deposits on the replacement property come directly from the exchange escrow account. The deposit is sent or wired to the Realtor, attorney, or title company. However, with a sheriff's sale you need cash (or a cash equivalent such as a bank check) right on the spot. There is no waiting for wires or mail. In the ideal exchange, it is highly preferable that the exchanger not handle any money at all so that there is no trace of "constructive receipt." Thus, we do not want the exchanger to first tender the cash and then be reimbursed from the escrow account. Any moneys from the escrow account directly to the exchanger could disqualify the entire exchange.

Here are recommendations, listed in order of preference:

1. The exchanger can draw the money in advance from the exchange escrow account with the bank check payable to the sheriff (or whomever, just *not* to the exchanger)

2. Here the exchanger may have to estimate. It is better to be over. Any excess could be directly returned to the escrow account. Have a person other than the exchanger tender the cash from his or her account; then this other person (not the exchanger) is reimbursed out of the exchange escrow account. The other person could be a Realtor, an attorney, or a friend—even a lineal relative. However it should not be the exchanger's spouse. It also should not be any other co-owners of the properties in the exchange.

3. The exchanger tenders the funds from his or her own account and is not reimbursed from the escrow account. The deposit is included as part of the exchange by way of a "paper" assignment of the deposit in the exchange documentation.

1031 Exchange Documents

Notice of Assignment with Qualifying Intermediary: One of the requirements of a 1031 exchange is that there be written notice of an assignment of the exchanger's rights into the replacement property agreement to the QI. This assignment is generally done by way of an addendum to the purchase agreement of the replacement property. The 1031 Exchange

Addendum and Assignment is signed by the exchanger, the seller, and the QI. (It could also be done in letter form.) With a sheriff sale, there generally is not a purchase/sale agreement. There will be a deed to the buyer, usually along with some other legal documents such as assignments of bids, affidavits, and so on. (each state varies). Moreover, as a seller, who is going to sign a "1031 Exchange" addendum? You probably will not get much cooperation here.

Recommendation

Fortunately there is a solution. The notice of assignment can be done in a letter form. Typically it would be a letter with the proper 1031 language. It would be prepared and signed by the QI with a CC to the exchanger. The letter will need to contain the legal description of the property. Therefore the exchanger should know ahead of time which properties he or she will bid on. The letters of assignment can then be prepared in advance of the sales. Once this is done, the exchanger can just hand the appropriate letter to the sheriff (or bank or attorney or all of them) at the foreclosure sale. (Additional copies should be taken.) Additional copies also should be sent certified mail with a return receipt. This procedure is not as clear cut as an addendum, but it technically should satisfy the IRS regulations requiring written notice of the assignment to the parties.

Settlement Sheet

In a typical real estate transaction (including a 1031), there are usually settlement sheets (or HUD-1s) summarizing the financial aspects of the transaction for both seller and buyer. When there is a 1031 exchange, the title company or closing attorney should be instructed to modify the settlement sheet so that it clearly reflects that a 1031 exchange has occurred. With a foreclosure, there is generally no such document, only the legal documents mentioned earlier.

1031 Tax Tip with Settlement Sheets

In an IRS audit involving real estate (including exchanges), the IRS agent generally looks to the settlement sheet as the nuclear document evidencing the transaction. Therefore it will benefit you to hire a title clerk to later prepare a 1031 settlement sheet (preferably with a HUD-1 form) from the foreclosure documentation. It should not be a significant cost (especially if you network with friendly title companies).

Public Auctions

Another way to get below-market buys in real estate is at voluntary auction sales—voluntary meaning this is not a foreclosure situation. The seller, by choice, has decided to use a professional auctioneer to sell the property at a public auction. The same 1031 problems that can happen with foreclosure sales can also happen at these auctions. Accordingly, you should follow the same planning recommendations.

Tip

Invest in the new updated third edition (2002) of the most comprehensive, creative guide on 1031s—*The 1031 Money Machine* by Albert Aiello. And now there is one of the most exciting, cutting-edge programs—Turbo-Exchange, the first do-it-yourself 1031 exchange forms and software kit also by Albert Aiello. To order these, call 1-888-544-4636 or 1-215-937-9207.

Other Tax Strategies for Your Foreclosure Properties

1. For your keepers, fully deduct all rental losses and avoid all IRS limitations on deducting losses per Goldmine Sections 25, 26, and 27.

2. For your keepers, see if you qualify for tax credits to rehab older or historic properties per Goldmine Section 20.

3. For your keepers, see if you qualify for tax credits for low-income housing per Goldmine Section 21.

4. For any losses on the sale of your foreclosure properties, follow the strategies in Goldmine Section 44. (I know you intend to make profits, and you will! But just in case!)

About ALBERT AIELLO

Since 1982, Albert Aiello has led hundreds of real estate tax seminars and offered an expanding list of creative publications. Consequently, he has developed the most powerful real estate tax reduction package in the country, saving real estate entrepreneurs hundreds and thousands of dollars in taxes.

Al is an active real estate investor. As both a residential and commercial realtor, Al had sold, listed, and managed millions of dollars worth of real estate. He also had his own tax practice specializing in real estate and IRS audit representation. However, he wanted something more creative, more challenging, and more rewarding, so he sold his practice to do what he really loves—conduct real estate seminars, write creative real estate publications, and actively invest in real estate.

Al also offers a powerful home study on tax reduction strategies for real estate investors. You can check it out on www.dealmakerscafe.com.

Following are examples of various types of contracts. Feel free to model your own after these.

Due-on-Sale Disclosure and Agreement

THIS DISCLOSURE AND AGREEMENT made this _____ day of _____, 20____, concerning the purchase of the property located at ____ by _____ ("Purchaser").

I have been made aware that my loan on the Property contains a "due on sale" clause, which means the lender has the right to call the entire loan due upon the transfer of the title to the Property.

I understand the loan will stay in my name until it is paid off or assumed by a future Purchaser.

I am aware that the above Purchaser has no intention of assuming said loan and that no promises have been made to me that the loan will be assumed or paid off. I agree to hold harmless the Purchaser or assigns shown on the attached agreement, or any future Purchaser in the event the loan is called due or goes into default for any reason.

The Purchaser has agreed to make up the back payments, if any payments are in arrears at the time of closing, only upon the resale of the property. No promises have been made to do so prior to that time. If Purchaser is unable to resell the property, I understand the payments may not be brought current and the property may go into foreclosure, in which case the Purchaser will be held harmless.

SELLER:

_____ (SEAL)
Signature

_____
Printed name

_____
Social Security number

Homeowner's Policy

Insured by: _____

Company's address: _____

Policy number: _____

Location of insured property: _____

Name of insured: _____

Please be advised that I have obtained a Management Company in Virginia Beach to collect rents, to be in charge of all insurance matters related to the Property, and to make all mortgage, insurance, and other payments due relative to the abovementioned Property. The Company is:

_____

_____

_____

Please add _____ as an additional insured to the policy on this property that I currently have with your insurance company. The policy should now be a landlord policy with a $_____ deductible.

Please send all future statements, correspondence, policies, and any other related information regarding this property to the Management Company shown above. Please make any future claim checks or refunds payable to the Management Company as well.

I hereby authorize you to release to the Management Company any and all information that they may require regarding this insurance policy.

Sincerely yours,

_____

Signature

_____

Printed name and Social Security number

Mortgage Account Change Letter

Mortgage company: _____

Loan number: _____

Property address: _____

Name of borrower: _____

Please be advised that I have retained a Management Company to collect rents, to be in charge of all loan matters related to the Property, and to make loan payments on the abovementioned Property. The Company is:

_____

_____

_____

Beginning with the payment due on _____, your payments will come directly from the Management Company.

Please send all future payment statements, yearly interest statements (1099s), coupons, coupon books, refunds for changes in escrow balance, correspondence, and any other related information regarding this property to the Management Company shown above.

I hereby authorize you to release to the Management Company any and all information that they may require regarding this mortgage loan.

Sincerely yours,

_____

Signature

_____

Printed name

_____

Social Security number

Special Power of Attorney

KNOW ALL MEN BY THESE PRESENTS:

That I, _____ (person giving power to sign) of _____ (city and state), have made, constituted, and appointed, and by these presents do make constitute and appoint _____ (person receiving power to sign) my true and lawful attorney-in-fact, for me and in my name, place, and stead, to execute and sign any real estate contract addendum, deed, related contract or agreement, bond, possession agreement, settlement statement, lease, mortgage document, or any other paper, form, or instrument necessary and incident to the placement, completion, settlement, and consummation of cash on property known as:

SEE ATTACHED EXHIBIT A LEGAL DESCRIPTION

and to furthermore make any necessary covenants, warranties, and assurances, and to do any and all acts and things necessary and incident to the purchase, sale, or refinance of said property.

This Power of Attorney shall not be terminated by my disability, nor shall there be any liability on any person, firm, or corporation relying on this Power of Attorney subsequent to my death, provided such person, firm or corporation has not received actual notice of my death.

And we hereby ratify and confirm all lawful acts done by my said attorney-in-fact by virtue hereof.

The effective date of this instrument shall be the _____ day of _____, 20__, and shall terminate on the settlement and completion of the purchase, sale, or refinance transaction.

Witness the following signature and seal this _____ day of _____, 20__.

Signature and Date

NOTARY INFORMATION

Contract to Purchase Subject to Existing Financing

THIS CONTRACT is made this _____ day of _____, 20__, by and between _____ (the "Purchaser"), GRANTEES, and _____ (the "Seller"), GRANTORS.

WITNESSETH:

That for and in consideration of the mutual promises and covenants contained herein, the Purchaser agrees to buy and the Seller agrees to sell for the price and upon the terms set forth below all that certain piece, parcel, or lot of land (together with any and all improvements thereon), located in _____, and briefly described as follows:

SEE ATTACHED EXHIBIT A FOR LEGAL DESCRIPTION

and further known and numbered as _____ (such property is sometimes referred to herein as the "Property").

The purchase price of the Property shall include, without limitation, all items currently in the premises, together with all improvements to include the _____.

I. Terms of Sale.

The total purchase price for the Property shall be the balance due on the mortgage current attaching to the property at the time of closing, which is approximately _____ _____ _____ **dollars and** _____ **cents** ($_____) (the "Existing Note"). Purchaser is purchasing the Property subject to said existing note, bearing interest at _____ per annum. Purchaser is not expressly assuming responsibility for the Existing Note. Seller agrees to make all payments on the Existing Note until _____, at which time Purchaser shall start making payments on the Existing Note.

By affixing their signatures hereto the Purchaser hereby agrees that its rights of ownership will be subject to all of the terms, provisions, and conditions of the Existing Note, including, without limitation, making monthly payments as and when due from and after _____. The Purchaser acknowledges that the Existing Note is a _____-year loan (with _____ years and _____ months remaining as of _____) with interest at the rate of _____% with a current monthly payment of principal and interest in the amount of $_____. The Purchaser also understands that amounts shall be added to the principal and interest amount of each monthly payment noted above and shall be held in escrow by the holder of the Existing Note for payment of real estate taxes and hazard insurance premiums as they come due and that sums required for the payment of said real estate taxes and hazard insurance shall be adjusted from time to time based upon anticipated increases in those charges and assessments, and Purchaser agrees that its rights of ownership are subject to the obligation to pay those increased escrow amounts as and when they become due by making increased monthly payments as required by the holder of the Existing Note. Purchaser's rights as to prepayment and his obligations including, but not limited to, payment of late charges as to such installments, shall be as provided in the Existing Note, and in that certain deed of trust securing such note on the Property, which deed of trust is recorded among the land records of the Clerk's Office of **COURT IN CITY AND STATE** (the "Clerk's Office") in **Deed Book** _____, **at page** _____. (Such note and deed of trust are sometimes referred to herein as the "Existing Note" and the "Existing Deed of Trust," respectively.)

So long as Purchaser is current in payments due under the Existing Note and Existing Deed of Trust all of the tax benefits of home ownership, including, without limitation, interest and tax deductions for income tax purposes, shall accrue to the benefit of the Purchaser, and Seller shall not attempt to claim all or any part of said benefits.

2. Contract Term.

This contract shall be binding upon the parties hereto until the occurrence of one of the following events which shall occur no later than _____:

(a) Purchaser's successful application to the Noteholder to obtain a release of liability upon the Existing Note/Deed of Trust on behalf of Seller.

(b) Purchaser's obtaining a release of liability on behalf of the Seller, either by obtaining a refinance loan or selling the Property to a third party Purchaser who is obtaining new financing.

3. Payments on Existing Note.

Purchaser's rights of ownership are subject to all of the terms, provisions, and conditions of the Existing Note, including, without limitation, making monthly payments as and when due from and after _____.

4. Real Estate Taxes, Assessments.

The Purchaser shall pay all real estate taxes, other governmental assessments with respect to the Property, and homeowner or condominium association assessments (if applicable).

5. Closing and Possession Date.

At closing, the Seller shall deliver to the Purchaser a fully executed General Warranty Deed in recordable form, with English Covenants of Title, and conveying title to the Purchaser and/or its assigns, subject to liens, encumbrances, restrictions, easements, and covenants of record, and subject to the Existing Deed of Trust or Mortgage. On and after the Possession Date and so long as Purchaser is not in default hereunder, unless otherwise agreed in writing, the Purchaser shall be entitled to full possession, use, and enjoyment of the Property. All expenses referred to herein must be paid to the settlement attorney, and this Agreement and all documents referred to herein must have been executed, acknowledged (as required), and delivered to the settlement attorney. It is agreed that the Possession Date shall be _____, 20___.

6. Attorney's Fees and/or Closing Costs.

The settlement attorney's charges and/or closing costs for this transaction shall be paid by the Possession Date, as follows:

(a) The Purchaser shall pay to his settlement agent any and all fees related to title examination, title insurance, preparation of documents (including this contract), and the cost of all other settlement services. The Purchaser also agrees to pay any and all settlement charges related to this transaction (other than any charge made by Seller's agent or attorney which Seller hereby agrees to pay), and Seller shall have no obligation to contribute to the payment of those costs.

(b) The Seller shall also pay any and all of the Buyer's closing costs associated with this transaction up to $_____.

7. Adjustments.

The parties agree that in lieu of prorations all mortgage payments and escrow accounts shall be current and pass gratis. Mortgage payments due after the possession date shall be paid by Purchaser.

8. Risk of Loss: Insurance.

Risk of loss as to the Property shall be borne by the Seller prior to the Possession Date. From and after such date, the Purchaser shall bear all risk of loss as to the Property and of liability for injury or damage to persons or property thereon. Purchaser shall continuously maintain or cause to be maintained a hazard insurance policy providing coverage of at least the unpaid principal balance of any outstanding liens with the mortgage company reflected as an additional loss payee.

9. Default by Purchaser.

Should the Purchaser default in any of the terms or provisions of this agreement, and remain in default for a period of thirty (30) days after receiving written notice from the Seller of such default, Seller may bring an action against Purchaser for any and all damages incurred by Seller by virtue of Purchaser's default, including, without limitation, attorney's fees and costs incurred.

10. Default by Seller.

Should Seller default in any of the terms or provisions of this agreement, and remain in default for a period of thirty (30) days after receiving written notice from the Purchaser of such default, Purchaser may bring an action against Seller for any and all damages incurred by Purchaser by virtue of Seller's default, including, without limitation, attorney's fees and costs incurred.

11. Termination.

Purchaser has the right to declare this agreement null and void at any time before the closing date. Upon said termination, neither party shall have any further liability to the other under this Agreement, except as otherwise expressly provided in this Agreement

12. Title.

Purchaser shall cause title to be examined prior to possession. It is understood that title to said property shall be good of record and in fact and Purchaser may purchase at time of possession of said property a title insurance policy insuring Purchaser's interest. If, after the examination of the title, the Purchaser determines any matters reported in the title report that would make title to the Property unmarketable or uninsurable under an ALTA owner's title insurance policy or that would adversely affect the use of the Property for its intended purpose in the reasonable opinion of Purchaser, the Purchaser may terminate this Agreement by giving Seller written notice thereof at any time prior to the closing date. Upon said termination, neither party shall have any further liability to the other under this Agreement. Seller shall have no obligation to cure any such defect in title.

13. Termite Certificate.

The Purchaser has the right to have the Property inspected for termite or other wood-destroying insect infestation or damage and structural moisture damage prior to closing at Purchaser's sole cost and expense. If the Purchaser determines that its inspections, investigations, and the like are unacceptable or unsatisfactory for any reason, the Purchaser may terminate this Agreement by giving Seller written notice thereof at any time prior to the closing date. Upon said termination, neither party shall have any further liability to the other under this Agreement.

14. Sellers' Warranty.

Sellers warrant that all plumbing, electric, heating, and air-conditioning systems which convey with the Property will be in working order on the Possession Date, and Purchaser reserves the right to make a walk-through inspection to determine their working order. All utilities necessary for the walk-through shall be provided by Seller.

15. Lender Documents.

As such, the Lender's records will continue to reflect the Seller as the owner of the Property and may also reflect the Seller's forwarding address for documentation purposes. The Seller hereby agrees that he will forward to the Purchaser at the Property address, or at such other address as the Purchaser may, from time to time, advise Seller in writing, any documentation received from the lender, including, without limitation, payment coupon books, escrow analyses, and year-end tax statements. Should Seller fail to forward Lender documentation as set forth above, and should said failure to forward result in financial damages suffered by the Purchaser, Seller shall be fully responsible for payment of such damages.

16. Maintenance of Property and Erection of Further Improvements.

During the continuance of this Agreement, the Purchaser shall keep the Property and any improvements now existing or hereafter erected in good repair and protected from the elements.

17. Time of Settlement.

Closing shall occur prior to _____ at the offices of Purchaser's Settlement Agent.

18. Prior Deed of Trust.

The Purchaser and the Seller acknowledge the fact that this Contract is subject to the provisions of the Existing Deed of Trust. The Purchaser acknowledges that the Existing Deed of Trust secures a loan and understands and acknowledges that recordation of the deed would give to the servicing mortgage company the right to call the loan, which would require Purchaser to immediately pay in full all sums still owing under the Existing Note and Existing Deed of Trust. Further, Purchaser acknowledges that he has reviewed the terms and conditions of said deed of trust, and notwithstanding the existence of said deed of trust, the Purchaser hereby agrees to accept and consummate the purchase of the Property in accordance with this Contract and the Escrow Agreement. The Purchaser and Seller further acknowledge that neither this Agreement nor the Escrow Agreement will alter the terms and conditions of the Existing Note and the Existing Deed of Trust and that this real estate transaction is subject to the terms of the Existing Note and the Existing Deed of Trust.

19. Partial Invalidity: Survival.

The invalidation for any reason of any portion hereof shall not cause this Contract to be invalidated in its entirety, but it shall survive any such failure of any part hereof.

20. Entire Agreement.

This Agreement contains the final and entire agreement between the parties, and they shall not be bound by any terms, conditions, statements, or representations, oral or written, not herein contained.

21. Waiver of Default.

No waiver or forbearance by any party hereto with respect to a default or breach by any other party shall constitute or be construed as a waiver of any subsequent default or breach.

22. Miscellaneous.

This Contract shall be binding upon and inure to the benefit of the parties hereto, their successors and assigns. Any reference to the masculine gender shall include the feminine and neuter, reference to the singular number shall include the plural, and vice versa, all as the context requires. The captions or headings are for convenience only and are not part of the substantive provisions hereof. This contract shall be construed according to the laws of the State of _____.

WITNESS the following signatures and seals:

Purchaser: _____
  Signature   *Date*   *Printed Name*

Seller: _____
  Signature   *Date*   *Printed Name*

EXHIBIT A

LEGAL DESCRIPTION

Physical Address: _____

Deed for Purchase or Sale

THIS DEED, made this _____ day of _____, 20__, by and between _____, Grantor, party of the first part, and _____, Grantee, party of the second part, whose address is: _____

WITNESSETH:

THAT, for good and valuable consideration, cash in hand paid by the party of the second part to the party of the first part, and other good and valuable considerations, the receipt whereof is hereby acknowledged, the said party of the first part does hereby bargain, sell, grant, and convey, with **GENERAL WARRANTY and ENGLISH COVENANTS OF TITLE,** unto the party of the second part, the following described property located at _____ _____, to wit:

LEGAL DESCRIPTION OF THE REAL PROPERTY

TAX INFORMATION

This conveyance is made expressly subject to all existing liens, mortgages, deeds of trust, judgments, encumbrances, conditions, restrictions, reservations, and easements of record, if any; but there is no intention by this reference to reimpose or to extend any of the same.

WITNESS the following signature and seal:

_____ (SEAL)

NOTARY INFORMATION

Assignment of Deed of Trust

THIS ASSIGNMENT, is made this _____ day of _____, 20__, by and between **SELLER OF DEED OF TRUST MORTGAGE**, hereinafter Grantor, party of the first part, and **BUYER OF DEED OF TRUST MORTGAGE**, hereinafter Grantee, party of the second part.

WITNESSETH:

FOR good and valuable consideration, the receipt of which is hereby acknowledged by the Grantor, the Grantor does hereby transfer and assign, without recourse, unto _____, Grantee, all of its right, title, and interest in and to that certain Deed of Trust dated _____ executed by **ORIGINAL GRANTOR** to _____, Trustee, and recorded in the Clerk's Office of the **COURT IN CITY AND STATE**, as instrument number _____ (or at Deed Book _____ at Page Number _____), together with the Deed of Trust Note dated _____ it was given to secure in the original principal amount of _____.

IN WITNESS WHEREOF, **SELLER OF DEED OF TRUST MORTGAGE** has caused this instrument to be executed by affixing its seal hereto this ____ day of _____, 20__.

SELLER OF DEED OF TRUST MORTGAGE

BY

NOTARY SEAL

DOCUMENT TAX INFORMATION

Payoff Authorization

Re: Borrower: _____

Property: _____

Loan number: _____

AUTHORIZATION TO RELEASE INFORMATION

This is to authorize your office and/or its agents to release to _____
any and all information pertaining to the payoff of the mortgage loan held by your
company on the captioned property.

Please immediately fax the payoff amount of the loan to _____.

_____

_____
Date

_____
Signature

_____
Printed name

_____
Social Security number

General Mortgage Information Authorization

AUTHORIZATION TO RELEASE INFORMATION

I hereby authorize you to release to:

_____

_____

_____

any and all information that they may require for the purpose of a credit transaction or loan transfer. This document may be reproduced for reference from more than one source, and I direct that a photostatic copy of this authorization be accepted with the same authority as the original.

Sincerely yours,

_____

Signature

_____

Printed name

_____

Social Security number

Disclosure and Agreement between Purchaser and Seller

THIS DISCLOSURE AND AGREEMENT made this _____ day of _____, 20__, by and between **BUYER OF REAL ESTATE SUBJECT TO EXISTING FINANCING** (the "Purchaser") and **SELLER** (the "Seller").

This transaction may be considered a disposition of residential property securing a loan, and therefore may require approval by the note holder prior to the closing of this transaction. Any Seller considering a sale in this manner should be cautioned that under such an arrangement he or she remains liable for repayment of the loan. Even if the agreement calls for the Purchaser to make payments directly to the note holder, the holder is not required to change its records, and the Seller is responsible for forwarding payment coupons and other information to the Purchaser. Depending on the particular circumstances of a case, a holder may agree to change the account address to read in care of the Purchaser, although the Seller must promptly advise the holder of any change in his or her address.

The Purchasers and Sellers acknowledge that they have read and understood the above language and realize that recordation of a deed into Purchasers prior to Purchasers obtaining a release of liability on behalf of Seller may result in the note holder calling all sums due under the Existing Note and Existing Deed of Trust immediately due and payable. Furthermore, Sellers understand that, notwithstanding the fact that the Contract calls for Purchasers to make monthly mortgage payments on behalf of the Sellers, the Sellers remain fully responsible for any default of the Purchasers, and, until the Purchasers provide Seller with a release of liability of eligibility, the note holder has the absolute right to proceed solely against the Seller for said default.

WITNESS the following signatures and seals.

PURCHASER:

_____ (SEAL)

Signature

_____

Printed name

SELLER:

_____ (SEAL)

Signature

_____

Printed name

NOTARY INFORMATION

Standard Contract to Purchase Real Estate: Buyer

1. I/we offer to purchase from Seller the following described real estate, together with all improvements thereon and all appurtenant rights, located at:

   Address: _____ City: _____

   County: _____ State: _____ Zip: _____

2. The purchase price is to be $_____ payable as follows: _____ down and the balance over _____ years at _____%, payable monthly.

3. The conditions of the Purchase are as follows:
   a. Subject to review, inspection, and written approval of my financial partner.
   b. Purchaser shall have the right to assign his/her interest in this contract prior to escrow.
   c. Seller agrees to allow purchaser to show property to prospective partners and clients prior to closing.

4. Is there an Addendum to this contract? Yes ____ No ____

5. Is this deal "All cash" or "Terms"? All cash _____ Terms _____

6. Possession is to be given on or before _____.

7. Seller agrees to pay all Taxes and Assessments up to and including the month of _____, 20___.

8. All closing costs and attorney's fees shall be paid by Seller.

9. Closing date shall be 90 days from the date of this agreement, with title to the above-described real estate to be conveyed by Warranty Deed with release of dower. Title is to be free, clear, and unencumbered, free of building orders, subject to zoning regulations of record, and except easements and restrictions of record. The Seller shall pay for and produce a valid title insurance policy protecting the Purchaser at closing.

10. This offer, when accepted, comprises the entire agreement of Purchaser and Seller, and it is agreed that no other representation or agreements have been made or relied upon.

11. This offer is to remain open for acceptance until _____.

Date: _____   Date: _____

Seller _____   Purchaser _____

Seller _____   Purchaser _____

Seller understands by signing this agreement that the Buyer is a real estate investor and may resell the property for a profit. Seller understands and agrees that the Buyer does not represent the Seller's interest.

Standard Contract to Purchase Real Estate: Seller

1. I/we offer to purchase from Seller the following described real estate, together with all improvements thereon and all appurtenant rights, located at:

   Address: _____ City: _____

   County: _____ State: _____ Zip: _____

2. The purchase price is to be $_____ payable as follows:

3. The conditions of the Purchase are as follows: Sold "As is."

4. Is this deal "All cash" or "Terms"? All cash _____ Terms _____

5. Possession is to be given on or before _____ (date of deed).

6. Seller agrees to pay all Taxes and Assessments up to and including the month of _____, 20___.

7. All closing costs and attorney's fees shall be paid by Purchaser.

8. Nonrefundable earnest money of _____ to be held by Seller.

9. Closing date shall be on or before _____, 20___, with title to the above-described real estate to be conveyed by Warranty Deed with release of dower.

10. This offer, when accepted, comprises the entire agreement of Purchaser and Seller, and it is agreed that no other representation or agreements have been made or relied upon.

11. This sale shall close by _____.

Date: _____ Date: _____

Seller _____ Purchaser _____

Seller _____ Purchaser _____

Disclaimer: the Purchaser understands and agrees by signing that the Seller does not represent the Buyers or their interests. This sale is contingent upon the Buyers being able to pass good title, which they may or may not have at this time.